Tiresias, a former commuter and civil servant, is currently compiling a modern Greek dictionary. He lives with his family near Oxford.

TIRESIAS

Notes from Overground

A Commuter's Notebook

PALADIN

Granada Publishing

Paladin Books
Granada Publishing Ltd
8 Grafton Street, London W1X 3LA

First published by Paladin Books 1984

A Granada Paperback Original

ISBN 0-586-08462-2

Reproduced, printed and bound in Great Britain by
Hazell Watson & Viney Ltd,
Aylesbury, Bucks
Set in Baskerville

Acknowledgments

I am grateful to the following for permission to reproduce extracts: Jonathan Cape Ltd and the estate of Arthur Koestler for *Darkness at Noon* and *Conversations with Claude Levi-Strauss* by G. Charbonnier, translated by John and Doreen Weightman; A. P. Watt Ltd and Miss D. E. Collins for G. K. Chesterton's 'A Ballade Of The First Rain' from *Collected Poems*; Faber and Faber Ltd for 'The Dry Salvages' from T. S. Eliot's *Four Quartets*; George Allen and Unwin for *J. R. R. Tolkien: a Biography* by Humphrey Carpenter; Deborah Rogers Ltd for *The Unquiet Grave* by Palinurus; A. P. Watt Ltd for 'The King' and *Kim* by Rudyard Kipling; Times Newspapers Ltd for the article by John Pudney in the *Sunday Times Magazine* of 28 January 1968.

This book is dedicated to
Gordon Grange of Basel
and
Paul Surman of Horspath

Only disconnect . . .

LITERARY LANDMARKS, No 7 Slough. Slough is a literary landmark. It ought not to be. Yet it does not earn its place in this
series only on the strength of Sir John Betjeman's searing
indictment:

> Come, friendly bombs, and fall on Slough,
> It isn't fit for humans now,
> There isn't grass to graze a cow,
> Swarm over, Death!

Betjeman could more appositely have written: " No
yard of soil fit to plough," because, as we clatter
through Slough station, we could see, two or three miles away,
if it wasn't for the factories in between, Stoke Poges church,
past which Thomas Gray's ploughman once wearily plodded.
Gray's *Elegy* makes solemn reading for all, but especially for
the commuter who every day participates in "the madding
crowd's ignoble strife."

Somewhere near Slough station the train bisects the path
Gray used to take between Stoke Poges and Eton. Somewhere,
in the middle of all these light industry, all these roads and
railway lines, beneath these lumbering jumbo jets, lies the
spot where the idea came to him for his *Ode on a Distant*

Commuter. Commuter. Commuter. Say it over and over again. A rude rune. An indecent incantation. The prisoner's sentence commuted to life imprisonment on a train. Strange verbal resemblance to another automaton, the computer. Confusion with it too. 'I am a computer.' 'Are you still computing?' 'Angry computers besieged the booking-office.' Holder of a commutation ticket. To commute. To change. To suffer a land change into something poor and commonplace. This rune, this incantation, an escape attempt.

A train of thought. Sometimes the couplings break. But all those worlds trundled to and fro every day. Rolled snowballs gathering material *en route*. Melting snowballs diminished by daily thaw.

After so many years I feel bludgeoned, made punch-drunk by a journey of over an hour, morning and evening. No commuter could write a novel. Have begun this Notebook as occupational therapy. But am not writing it up on the train.

The train. For the commuter there is only one train. He travels on dozens of different trains which he can momentarily distinguish by certain details. By particular passengers. By type of passenger – e.g. Knightsbridge shoppers. By ticket-collectors. Buffet-car staff. (Not by drivers, whom he never sees.) By position of heating handles and light switches – he has to know where these are and how to work them to survive. By quaint labels telling him that the coach is made from lacewood or crown elm. By tidemark on windows. Stains on tables. Slashes in seats.

Graffiti: '6 foot 2, eyes of blue, Jimmy Holton's after you', 'Penzance Skins'. But he makes all his journeys, lives all too much of his life, on one train, *the* train.

The commuter – *l'homme moyen de notre époque*. The anti-hero of our age. More than the soldier, the nuclear physicist, the political prisoner or the starving child, he indicates where we've gone wrong.

This morning, not only a level crossing barrier failure at Ascot-under-Wychwood, but also a points failure at – where else? – Maidenhead. We sat for three quarters of an hour. Some ordered brandies. A. did Zen exercises to flex his wrists. Girl opposite offered alternative of massage. A. accepted. *Girl* then needed brandy.

Yes – only one train. Yet the commuter himself changes constantly. Fare forward, travellers! A different I catches the same train each day. The sleepy rhythm of a hundred hours. Years largely wasted, the years of *l'entre deux gares*. Ridiculous the waste sad time stretching before and after.

November to March the hard crown of the commuter's year. Fogs. Storms. Darkness morning and night – a kind of hooding torture. Weekends remind him what his home looks like. Just as he savours it, Monday strikes again.

MYSTERY 1
The tent in midwinter by swollen Thames. At first shipshape. Then sagging. One day collapsed, with boots, socks, bedding scattered. We shall never know why. Like television the train shows commuting viewers pictures of a reality they cannot approach. The river's tent is broken . . .

Commuters are all Palinuri, dead but unburied in the ebb and flow, awaiting release from limbo.

OVERHEARD 1
'The weekend is the only time I live.'

Like hospital patients we compare symptoms and scars, recount operations. What happened to me on the night of the fog / crash / derailment / snow / go-slow / strike / signal-failure. What did you do on the morning of the level crossing malfunction / the theft of two miles of copper wire / the fire / breakdown / frozen points / bomb-scare / concrete slabs on the line / snapped coupling? We got out and walked / drank the bar dry / caught a Mickey Mouse at Slough / sat in the dark when the batteries went flat / ran a gauntlet of flame / went round by Perivale on a shuttle / raved at the guard / shared a cream cake intended for a dinner party / played Twenty Questions and Consequences . . .

We share patients' addiction to minutiae. Like them we use trivia to keep reality at bay. A lot of our conversation based on the timetable. We weigh the merits and demerits of the 0700, the 0712, the 0735 etc. etc. We discuss changes in the rolling-stock. We comment when the buffet-car staff of the 1815 move to the 1715. We speculate when the train travels on an unaccustomed track. This saves us from mentioning religion or philosophy or literature or death or, worst of all, life.

One man holds forth about the readings on his barometer and rain-gauge. Another carries a writing-pad which he fills with items like 'Hazy, light NE wind, W. Crusader from Padd 100369 05 mins 31 secs late at Read'. The latter at least 35 and wears cavalry twill trousers. Many claim (as if some kind of virtue) expert knowledge of all railway intricacies from the classification of locomotives to the working of an electronic signalling system. 99.9% of the talk on the train consists of little, verifiable facts. Facts about business, sport, cars, advertising, money, houses, gardens, family, holidays. We cling to these facts. We make fetishes of them. Few realise, fewer still would admit, that these eagerly bandied facts are utterly valueless and useless. Pinchbeck Monopoly money.

When discharged, I hope to smuggle this document past the

barrier. If 'They' discover it, 'They' will destroy it, and I shall lose remission of sentence.

OBIT 1
Only an early riser knows
Weight of dew on sprig of rose.

Trucks with the fishy names: Herring, Grampus, Dogfish, Salmon, Ling, Sole, Haddock, Prawn, Sturgeon, Mermaid, Shark, Whiting, Catfish, Minnow, Sealion, Lamprey, Tunney, Starfish, Whale, Turbot.

Trucks with ungainly names: Vanfit, Hyfit, Lowfit, Medfit, Minfit, Conflat, Tube, Shochigh, Shocvan, Carflat, Hybar, Boplate, Pipe, Weltrol, Bocarp, Rectank, Mogo.

Trucks with the functional names: Coal, Fruit, Banana, Ore, Sand, Stone, Grain, Slate Powder, Cement, Oil, Bitumen, Steel.

Rolling-stock which defies categorisation: Iron Ore Tippler, Track Testing Car, Sleeping & Messing Van, Bogie Bolster, Hop, Broad Clyst, Barrow, Plate, Loriot, Reach Wagon, Trenching Unit, Ballast Cleaner, Gane, Siphon, Pallet Van, Cinema Coach, Express Parcels, Open, Clo.

Legends on rolling-stock: Condemned, Enparts, Denparts, No Naked Light, For Use On Merry-Go-Round Air-Braked Trains Only, Shunt With Care, Not To Be Hump Shunted, Not To Be Loose Shunted, Replace Chain Pocket Lids, Long Chord Levelling And Lining System, Experimental Clear Roof, For Spoil Only, House Coal Concentration, Do Not Part.

I spy: A.L. Rowse, Sheridan Morley, Lord Longford, Brian Aldiss, Peter Levi, John Wain, the Bishop of Damaraland, Humphrey Carpenter, the Lord Mayor of Oxford, James Cobban, John Sparrow, the retired Archbishop of Canterbury. Transitory visitors from outer space.

ANTI-KONTAKION 1

A curse on the train. Phallus spilling semen in precocious ejaculation. Greenhouse killing humans by ferocious suffocation. Anathema sit.

Sex seldom discussed. Male commuters hardly ever talk about women as we might in a pub. We cannot forget them because we see some very beautiful ones (birds of passage, for truly beautiful women scarcely ever commute). But even when we sit next to them or opposite them, we know that they are unattainable, so we try to ignore both their physical presence and the idea of Woman.

Some women, alas, misguidedly board the train provocatively dressed, perhaps displaying thigh or cleavage. They do not realise that a man when he commutes is commuted. He becomes delicate, sensitive. He may show no signs of being disturbed, but inwardly he suffers. If they do realise this, they are sadists whose challenge is tantamount to flaunting themselves before the inmates of Bedlam.

OVERHEARD 2

'So you must be Sister Augusta. It's a small world.'

The newspaper – our opiate, our anodyne. In the morning anyone travelling without one invites suspicion. Anyone who speaks during the sacred hour of the newspaper shows himself to be an ignorant boor, the sort of person who might try to give all his neighbours the kiss of peace at an early morning communion service. On the other hand, cannot understand why, in the evening, people buy papers full of small advertisements and incomplete details of the next day's racing.

I always tackle the crossword puzzle first. Believe I have my priorities right (insofar as anyone who spends at least two hours a day in trains can be supposed to have his priorities right). Could happily dispense with the rest of the rag, given a crossword guaranteed to take me at least an hour to solve. The crossword alone offers truth – perfect, Euclidean truth, the search for which can satisfy and fill the mind to the exclusion of all else. My grounding in the Classics and

English literature at last comes into its own. All that education, which seemed so pointless, was aimed towards this solving of the daily conundrum. Clearly our mentors did not explain this at the time, even when we questioned them, because they knew we lacked the maturity required of initiates of the mystery.

Open coaches resemble public hospital wards. (Private patients travel First Class.) A mixture of cases. Casualties. Incurables. Schizophrenics. The lot. Most of us suffer from terminal illnesses contracted as a result of over-exposure to termini. Paddingtonian carcinoma.

The way announcers address the passenger-patients strengthens the hospital analogy. They employ any euphemism – 'operational difficulties', 'locomotive failure', 'staffing problems', 'adverse weather conditions' – rather than divulge the true nature of the disease, rather than reveal the feverish reading on the thermometer.

These notes, to be explicit, concern daily commuting on what is at present known as Western Region, between Oxford and Paddington. Many of us do this, yet, when commuting is mentioned, we do not spring to people's minds. I trust that these shored fragments demonstrate that other commuters exist – if our life can be called an existence – besides those who live in that commuter belt which holds up the pin-striped trousers of the City, those who were undone when Eliot observed them flowing over London Bridge. We salute them, more as cousins than as brothers. We, the unrecognised commuters.

Excitedly I pointed out a rainbow redeeming Slough. No fellow-passenger turned to look.

Our journey never lasts less then an hour, often an hour and a quarter, sometimes longer still. We travel on the same trains as ordinary folk whose occasions take them to London, Hereford, Swansea, Worcester, Bristol, Cheltenham. Our lot compares both favourably and unfavourably with that of our Southern and Eastern Region cousins. We have corridors, tables, buffets, restaurants, clean lavatories with soap, towels and scalding water. We seldom stand or are cramped. But they have the inestimable advantage of time.

They endure a brief, undisguised ordeal. We, lulled by the trappings of civility which surround our journey, are deceived, tricked into selling our lives. Indeed, we do not even sell them, for we pay several hundred pounds a year train-geld to be hostages of the train.

> Desire! Desire! I have too dearly bought,
> With price of mangled mind, thy worthless ware.
>
> (Sidney)

How escape the contagion of the world's slow train? Watch out! I may be joking with clenched teeth (Dostoyevsky) – and when I clench my teeth I may be joking.

OBIT 2

A later comer passing by
Imagines brambles always dry,
Unburdened, pointing to the sky.

SPELT FROM ROGER'S THESAURUS

Nouns associated with commuting: accidie, angst, cafard, catalepsy, catatonia, ennui, hebetude, kenosis, narcosis, neomort, noia, spleen, taedium vitae, zombie.

Adjectives describing commuters: addled, banjaxed, bludgeoned, blunted, brain-washed, comatose, dazed, de-humanised, deracinated, desiccated, doped, dulled, etiolated, fragged, hypnotised, mesmerised, punch-drunk, sapped, stultified, stupefied, swinked, train-sick, train-washed.

Phrases: conveyed in suspended animation, shotten her-ring, suffering from over-train/train-lag/train-reaction, a living vegetable, victim of the train-drain.

Small child in stationary train at Paddington: 'This is our journey, Dad, isn't it?'

While policemen grow younger, train-spotters grow older.

Persians in pyjamas lead their own lives on my train.

In the winter dusk, at successive stations, we peer out to see wives waiting behind steering-wheels, children scuffling in back seats. Daddies descend and are met. Each set of participants knows only of its own little scene. None think of the others they will never meet. For those of us travelling further, the train links dozens of these poignant reunions in a parody of Philip Larkin's *The Whitsun Weddings*. Repetition emphasises futility. Each welcomed father ought not to learn of the existence of dozens of others along the line, any more than a prisoner should hear of the execution of his fellows. The train rudely unites episodes meant to be separate. It defiles the sacred. A rapist, it employs junction and coupling by force. It makes us omniscient gods before turning our knowledge to ashes.

Scene: a compartment for eight with a person in each corner. Enter a family of four who seat themselves in the remaining places. Comments one: 'Phew! This train is crowded!' Examine and discuss.

TRAIN GAME 1

People try to conceal what they are reading. They realise that you can read a man like a book through his choice of reading matter. The game lies in spotting titles or headings by fair means and foul. First instalment of examples gleaned: The Geometrical Exploration of the Cube and Sphere, Life and Other Contingencies,* Civil Service Motoring, Throttle Techniques, Procurement Weekly, Dying.

In the evenings those who do not sleep or drink read anything and everything. N. once observed: 'There's a great Trollope revival on this train.' The trains between Oxford and Paddington convey to and fro dozens of scholars *manqués*. The tracks are bedded on unfinished theses and third-class degrees. What we read reflects this. We want to prove not only that we are not wasting our time, but also that the advantages of a commuter's life outweigh those of

* (Subsequently discovered that Anthony Thwaite had spotted this one too and used it in a poem.)

14

the academic rat-race. But the man holding Plato open in front of him – he has not turned a page for half an hour – secretly hankers after the latest Dick Francis. *The Republic*, even in translation, disturbs him. Sour grapes. Sour grapes, both our pretensions to learning and our pretences to despise it. Nothing but sour grapes.

'When me they fly I am the wings.' Commuters journey from nowhere to nowhere. We delude ourselves if we imagine that the train provides a means of transport from A to B and back again. Or that it offers escape from boring job or unhappy home. The train travels in a vicious circle. We suppose ourselves free agents while all the time it possesses us, making us dance to its monotonous tune.

Spring surprised us, coming up behind Didcot power-station in a flurry of snow. British Summer Time. Four months have passed since last we travelled home by daylight. At a stroke the landscape is unveiled. Greenness and floods, new buildings and fresh tillage, show us how man and nature have spent the long undercover period, while we have festered and fusted.

Dear Notebook – indeed. After only a few pages you have become a presence in my life. When – as I frequently do – I think of you, I visualise you as already complete. I think you more than I write you. You have transformed my commuting. I now shun the company of train acquaint-ances. I sit in carriages where I am not known, looking eagerly out of the window, hoping to spot some outlandish truck-name or other anomaly for my – your – our – collection. I find material for you everywhere. This tends to make me self-conscious. But I count self-consciousness an asset for the commuter, who all too easily lapses into an oblivious trance. I am excited to find you assuming a life of your own, taking me over, a willing acolyte. You provide immediate effective therapy, and an encouraging intimation of a not too remote total salvation. With you as an ally I can fight the evil hypnotist.

Inscriptions and nomenclature of rolling-stock add up to a foreign language which I have no wish to learn. In this picturesque country I remain by choice an ignorant tourist. A dude on safari I gawp in fascination secure behind plate glass. What shall it profit a man to be able to identify a merry-go-round train when he sees one? I seek poetry, not information.

> For Gods works are like him, all infinite;
> And curious search, but craftie sinnes delight.
> (Fulke Greville)

ANTI-KONTAKION 2

A curse on the train. Maggot tunnelling in the cosmic apple. Television studio full of unreal people. Chained library of never-opened books. Mouldering scrolls of wisdom in a cave where no one looks. Anathema sit.

Season of floods. Swans swim on fields where worms drown. I have ridden my bicycle on Hinksey Reservoir beside the railway. With my mates I careered over the thick, unslippery ice in games confederate. I suppose those swans experience a similar *frisson* as they float on land.

I see this Notebook sometimes as akin to the log-book of a manned space mission – intrinsically boring, but exciting because it offers evidence that a man has done something dull, yet remarkable, and lived to tell the tale. The public and posterity demand that whatever man does, however tedious, should be recorded. He has made fewer moon flights than commuter journeys; yet, while the former have been exhaustively documented, the latter have scarcely been chronicled at all. I aim to repair this omission, to tell the world about conditions within the swaying module, about the gravitational forces which play havoc with the commuter's metabolism, about life in the void. How we overcome the problems of breathing, eating, drinking, sleeping, urinating, defecating, even occasionally ratiocinating, as we hurtle through space. How – What's that? Hello, Control. Do you read me? I am GO for Paddington. I remain bright-eyed and bushy-tailed. Roger and out.

OBIT 3

Day after day, inch after inch,
As clanks out on a well-oiled winch
An anchor chain, link by slow link,
Insights like these taught him to think.

Like the Bruce's spider I am trying to spin deliverance out of my own entrails. Even in a dark cave such an effort could lead to salvation. Accidie and spiritual death ensue only when one makes no attempt at all.

Rabbits. *Landtrain Up*? If rabbits can be anthropomorphised, I see no reason why they could not be portrayed as commuters – or, indeed, why commuters could not be depicted as rabbits. In a sequel I might represent British Rail as a monstrous ursine god exacting a tribute of human souls from its terrorized subjects. After that I could write about a maniac engine-driver who has undergone train-surgery and does not realise that he is paranoid. But no. That way lie pomposity and lethal seriousness. I seek to salvage my self-respect, not to write a best-seller.

But rabbits do feature in our commuting lives. We see them from the train, especially near Didcot. Some perch outside their burrows on the steep sides of the cutting. Others swarm in a meadow beside a wood. A black one lives, apparently alone, in a field with some geese. It cheers us to behold them. We watch for them, nudging one another like children and crying: 'O look at the rabbits!' or observing: 'Not many rabbits out this evening, are there?'

For many months there travelled with us a girl who claimed fame by being Britain's only female stamp auctioneer. She particularly loved the rabbits. She even liked to be woken up if there was a good cuniculine turn-out. When she gave up commuting to get married, we presented her, at a breakfast party on the 0817, with various items connected with trains all in a garish paper carrier-bag on which two rabbits were driving a blue steam locomotive.

Interesting that some designer – a commuter himself perhaps – had conjured up this picture of an NUR where the R stood for Rabbits. Rabbits seem pleasantly ridiculous.

They lend themselves to fantasy. They recall the true rabbit classics – Brer Rabbit, the White Rabbit in *Alice*, Peter Rabbit, Little Grey Rabbit – and, through them, our childhood. They indicate a possible escape route. No wonder commuters regard them with such delight and such yearning.

In Greek the word for 'transport' is *metaphora* which also means 'metaphor'. The train constitutes one extended metaphor conveying an inexhaustible supply of lesser ones. It is a metaphor-transporter or a metaphor of metaphors. A three-dimensional mobile metaphor for metaphor itself.

Sometimes catch trains which stop at the more truly commuter stations between Oxford and Paddington, and so can observe the people who travel from these points. They seem a different breed from the Oxford regulars.

They are no better or worse than us. All commuters are equally damned – though perhaps those who realise that the strait and narrow permanent way leads to perdition, yet still refuse to forsake it for the salvation of the primrose path that obliquely climbs out of the cutting, those of us who *know* yet will not act, will receive harsher penalties on the Day of Judgement.

The difference between us and them lies in the fact that these passengers are rootless. They come from places with no history, no culture. From houses containing only coffee-table books and volumes bound in tooled plastic. They smell of lotions. They often wear beards and smoke pipes. They give the seat a perfunctory brush of the hand and hitch up their expensive coat-tails before sitting down. They are the go-getters. They all look alike. An inscrutable race.

Few commuters wipe condensation off windows. When we pass or are passed by another train, perhaps ten coaches long, it no longer surprises me to spot only two or three panes with cleaned areas, eskimo fishing-holes, in the entire length of the train. Personally I do not scruple to improve visibility with great sweeping movements of my sleeve. A little extra wear and tear on my suit seems a small price to pay for some of the sunrises and frostscapes revealed by my efforts.

We think of the railway as a straight line. In fact it changes direction several times. The parallax of the rising sun brings this home to us. We see it first away to our left, over Wittenham Clumps. Half an hour later, far to our right, it hovers, huge and menacing, above the conning-tower of Windsor Castle, sharing the sky with jets from Heathrow. It amuses me to catch juxtaposed the two circles of the sun's orient disc and the round red NO SMOKING sign pasted to the window (the old triangular stickers are dying out); or to go a step further and actually to cover the former with the latter. The sun totally eclipsed by a NO SMOKING sign – a rare portent.

MYSTERY 2

One evening, passing a First Class compartment, noticed two of the waiters attending to a young woman who seemed to be throwing a fit of hysterics. Solicitously they were helping her to drink a plastic cupful of railway coffee. A little later, when I repassed the compartment, the waiters were gazing in some alarm at the woman who now lay supine on the seat, motionless, her pupils threatening to disappear. Post hoc *(the coffee) not necessarily* propter hoc, *but grounds for instant suspicion all the same.*

Brisez la machine. Who said that? Not a Luddite slogan. 'Ignore the vehicle' means roughly the same, I think. (Not sure who said that, either.) It certainly applies in a commuting situation, as they say. The train, the machine – *ex qua* may some *deus* materialise to save us in the nick of time – equals a container. For some a tangible prison; for others an almost invisible aquarium. A train-container as opposed to a container train. Whether prison or aquarium it needs breaking.

Those who feel incarcerated have more chance of smashing their way out. Those who, like captive goldfish, swim happily in circles, unaware of the transparent constricting bowl, may never try to escape. They have been insidiously conditioned to accept. *Pour vraiment briser la machine il faut la quitter.* A fatal mistake to believe you can transcend the train and continue commuting in a state of sublime levitation. No, if you achieve the first stage (perhaps through some sustained act of creation), the next stage is total renunciation, the clean break.

By Jove, we commuters have the Dunkirk spirit all right. Amongst us the humour of the trenches lives on. We thrive on adversity. Agatha Christie might have had us in mind when she wrote:

... the English *are* rather odd that way. Even in war, so much prouder of their defeats and their retreats than of their victories. Foreigners can never understand why we're so proud of Dunkirk. It's the sort of thing they'd prefer not to mention themselves. But we always seem to be almost embarrassed by a victory – and treat it as though it weren't quite nice to boast about it. And look at all our poets! The Charge of the Light Brigade, and the little Revenge went down in the Spanish Main. It's really a very odd characteristic when you come to think of it.

(*They Do It with Mirrors,* p. 104)

We rejoice when a guards' dispute or a minor derailment causes utter confusion. We enjoy the occasion itself, the camaraderie of the regulars, the discomfiture of casual travellers caught up in the chaos. These last, as we stand shoulder to shoulder generating a splendid fug in the only operative train, make remarks such as: 'They should all be horsewhipped!' and 'What this country needs is a dictatorship.' A girl faints. She has not room to collapse gracefully, so she remains slumped on her feet. We enjoy the occasion. In the days to come we shall no less enjoy comparing experiences. These defeats and retreats sustain us. When a train runs on time, that constitutes a kind of victory, and it is boring, even, as Agatha Christie says, embarrassing. Of course we prefer to forget about it while we revel in surviving the setbacks. Is that really so very odd?

DIALOGUE 1

Man: 'Do you think with all these strikes and so on, that Britain is going down the drain?'

Self: 'No.'
End of dialogue. The train lurches impassively onward.

A small comfort. Oxford, although a city, for some unsearchable reason does not qualify for the latest Inter-City trains. These have small tinted windows which cannot be opened; artificial temperature which cannot be adjusted; spring-loaded doors, symplegades which shut automatically with a loud thump; and painful strip lighting which always stays on and whines like a distant dentist's drill. They make it impossible either to hear station announcers or to bid friends farewell. They resemble modern crematoria, even, in some cases, having piped musak to sing you to your rest. They have been appropriately named. They do indeed inter their passengers. A recent poster reads: 'Inter-City – the easy way to go'. (Had already written the above when, one day, *The Times* crossword offered the clue: 'Inter-City (4)'. It took me no time at all to fill in: 'Bury'!)

John Pudney (*Sunday Times* Magazine 28/1/68) wrote:

In England, at the outset of Victoria's reign, the masses moved hardly at all. Travel was a luxury for the well-to-do: for the poor it was only undertaken in dire necessity. By the turn of the century, transportation was for all and even the least privileged citizens could contemplate travel for pleasure. There were misgivings about this. The Duke of Wellington had deplored the notion of railways on a national scale as 'they would encourage the lower classes to move about'.

Those were the days! What has happened now is that the middle classes, the *nouveaux pauvres*, are not encouraged to move about, but are forced to do so by dire necessity. *Mobile vulgus sumus*. By the year 2000, with any luck, the Wheel of Fortune, whether flanged or encased in pneumatic rubber, will have turned again, and we shall all be able to stay at home. How wonderful to live moving 'hardly at all'!

Newspapers feature so largely in commuters' lives. They survive by perpetuating two myths – that they themselves matter, and that London is the centre of the world. 'The more you think about it, the more you need X newspaper' declares an advertisement. It risks self-defeat, because the more you think about it, the more you realise that you need no newspaper. Indeed, the more you think, the less you need any kind of distraction. Fortunately for newspaper proprietors commuting conditions discourage rational thought.

We rush to buy newspapers in the morning, feel disoriented if they cannot be obtained, yet at the end of the journey many of us abandon them, and the unscrupulous can, and do, walk the length of the train gathering enough palliative pulp to last them through the working day. (Pity the cleaners on the days when *The Times* has one of its supplements on Bradford or Outer Mongolia.)

Freedom of the press is a myth of convenience on a par with Athenian democracy. What we need, commuters more than most, is freedom *from* the press.

OBIT 4

At first he revelled in his mind,
But gradually began to find
Life more elusive, till he felt
Unreal existence start to melt
Into an insubstantial haze
Of interludes in others' days.

LITERARY LANDMARK 1, OXFORD STATION

Max Beerbohm's Zuleika Dobson *(1911) opens thus:*

That old bell, presage of a train, had just sounded through Oxford station; and the undergraduates who were waiting there . . . struck a sharp note of incongruity with the worn boards they stood on, with the fading signals and grey eternal walls of the antique station which . . . does yet whisper to the tourist the last enchantments of the Middle Age.

He even goes on to mention 'the first class waiting-room'!

Today's installation says nothing to the tourist or to anyone else, unless it be the words of the prophet written on the subway wall: 'Oxford will die at Fratton'.

MYSTERY 3
FAR AWAY IS CLOSE AT HAND IN IMAGES OF ELSEWHERE

Beautifully lettered in large bold white capitals, this graffito appeared on a wall near Paddington one Christmas. The authorities must have decided that it was neither subversive nor obscene, because they allowed it to remain while obliterating carefully and completely a series of slogans, such as KILL THE PAGAN HAG ABORTION, which had appeared some months earlier. After several years it still stands out clearly, adorned here and there with tendrils of ivy. (Alas, no longer – see below.)

I imagine some poet, living perhaps in one of the nearby tenements, suddenly coming up with this line, considering it too good to be wasted, too good even to take its place in a mediocre poem, and deciding to present it to the widest possible audience.

It has made some of us commuters uneasy. With KILL THE PAGAN HAG ABORTION we knew where we were. With FAR AWAY IS CLOSE AT HAND IN IMAGES OF ELSEWHERE we feel suspicious. What does it mean, anyway? Is it a line of original poetry? Is it a seminal quotation from some master or guru? Does it have any connection with drugs? Does it simply mean that when you look at a travel poster it reminds you of last year's holidays? Is it code? Every time we pass it, a whiff of disturbing culture penetrates the train's philistine carapace.*

ANTI-KONTAKION 3
A curse on the train. Python that hypnotises. Boa constrictor that pulverises. Chancery Court luring men into sorrow. Favourable judgement deferred till tomorrow. Anathema sit.

Didcot has a kind of Red Indian reservation for survivals from the steam age of the Great Western Railway. Sometimes we glimpse dispossessed engines puffing wistfully behind their wire mesh fence. Occasionally they are allowed out for long runs. When this happens people flock to vantage-points along the route in order to watch, wave, and even cheer. I refuse to indulge in irrational nostalgia, but cannot refrain from observing that nobody waves at diesel

---

* See p. 137, for a new aspect of this mystery.

locomotives. Indeed, some youths feel impelled to throw stones at them, a sacrilege seldom if ever committed against steam engines.

OVERHEARD 3

Man travelling from Tilehurst (a mile or two further from Paddington than Reading is): 'I've been commuting for twenty years from Reading, and I've only just discovered that I can save quarter of an hour by catching the train at Tilehurst.'

(Assume that he goes to work on an average of 220 days per year. That's 440 journeys per annum. 440 × 15 × 20 = 132,000 minutes = 2200 hours = 91 days and 20 hours unnecessarily spent in travelling. A small unspectacular tragedy.)

Arrived at Didcot one evening to hear announcer saying: 'Passengers for Oxford will proceed by coaches which are waiting in the station forecourt.' Enjoyed being thus jolted out of my rut. We zoomed along the new Abingdon bypass through countryside once familiar to me, but now the only landmark I could recognise was Shippon church. The great road gave everything a strange perspective.

Road and rail – the traditional adversaries. Images of stagecoaches racing with trains. Now they are uneasily reconciled. Yet whoever heard of special train services being laid on when a road was blocked?

I took pleasure in the unexpected bus ride, but could not bear to commute daily by road. If the train did not exist I should stay at home. Have been half in love with the easeful train. Therein lies one of its dangers. I find it too congenial – an insidious drug to which my season ticket registers me as an addict. Must break the habit *soon* or it will be too late for rehabilitation. Can someone please put me in touch with Commuters Anonymous?

A not-so-superficial analogy: From time to time 'They' arbitrarily and without warning switch a train to a different platform, or assemble the constituent carriages in another order. When sudden changes like these occur, bewildered commuters scurry desperately hither and thither. So do ants scatter when a big boot disrupts their ordered comings and goings.

Animated scenes at Didcot one evening. A diesel multiple unit headed for Oxford stood at Platform 3. But it was not the scheduled connection for the express we had just left on Platform 1. It was a delayed earlier train. Its doors stood open. Passengers were climbing aboard. Passengers who, according to the timetable, did not exist. So the guard blew his whistle. The train moved off. People staggered and even fell. One elderly man with a walking-stick, caught with one foot on the platform and one on the train, was only saved because three or four young men grabbed him and hauled him in. Much shouting and protesting. Reluctantly the train stopped again, having moved only a few yards. End of incident. Can see the appeal of a complicated model railway layout in the attic – no pesky passengers to mess up the system.

MYSTERY 4

Not far from Paddington, beside the track, isolated on the edge of waste ground where they burn old motor cars, stands a small white-painted building with its name affixed to the front: DORMAR HOUSE. It appears to be the headquarters of some business or other. Had always vaguely supposed the name to have some connection with dormir. *After two and a half years' commuting I suddenly realised one day that DORMAR is RAMROD backwards. So?*

The train offers scope for indulgence of moods. Sometimes I like to play the recluse by sitting in a different carriage. Can be almost certain of seeing no one I know because, in general, a commuter travels in the same coach, often in the same seat, every day. Thus I pass the journey in meditation among strangers. Perhaps such behaviour – as some of my commuting cronies assert – brands me as peculiar. But we need to cultivate peculiarities to survive. I am a thinking drinker, a mute contemplative gossip, a gregarious hermit. I take the A and not A train. I pray: Let me not go sane!

'They' offer us no distractions. Gone the period photographs of Torquay and Mallaig which adorned the compartments of childhood. 'They' provide us only with mirrors whose silver linings hold threatening clouds.

Panic! Man in opposite corner seat, about my age, spectacles, scarred face, two silver bracelets, SCRIBBLING in an exercise book. Can see it's continuous prose, but can't read a word. Has he discovered the secret? Will his Commuter's Notebook take the world by storm? My absurd jealousy surprises me. Fame is not supposed to be the spur. Let 'em all come. Let every commuter write a Notebook. They will all differ, as witnesses' accounts of an accident differ. They will all contribute to the total picture. They will all fortify and comfort their writers. Then, when each man has finished his Notebook, let him scatter it page by page the whole length of the line on his last journey; or let him flush it down the lavatory when passing through Slough; or let him deposit it in the booking-hall of his home station along with his season ticket as an *ex voto* in gratitude for his escape; or let him publish and be saved.

'They' try to glamorise diesel engines, to endow them with spurious individuality, by slapping on their tinny sides weighty name-plaques: Western Thunderer, Titan, North Star etc. This fools nobody. If only 'They' would abandon this absurd pomposity and bring a little merriment into travellers' lives by painting the locomotives bright colours and giving them more suitable names, such as Western Rattletrap, Slowcoach, White Elephant ... But humour does not penetrate public undertakings like the railways, which are run with a funereal seriousness more appropriate to the other sort of undertaking.

Have heard it alleged that commuters *qua* commuters have no proper identities; that successive waves advance, do battle, die or retire, and are as if they had never been, unmourned, unmissed, unloved – unaneled, indeed, like Palinurus. This may apply in some areas but, thank God, it does not obtain on our line. We care about one another; notice absences; rejoice together; commiserate with sufferers. We know some of our fellow-commuters' names, and even go so far as to arrange social meetings off the train. When one of our number leaves the train, we remember him, exchange news about him, remain in touch with him.

This all happens naturally. Heaven forbid that we should form a club or association. In lack of organisation lies our hope of retaining a little humanity.

DIALOGUE 2

Women, seeing me looking out of window at floods, hares, four flying geese: 'Have you got a paper?'
Self: 'Why, yes.'
Woman: 'Oh good. I was afraid you hadn't got a paper. I know it can throw you out for the whole day if you don't get one. When I saw you looking out of the window I thought . . .'
Self: 'No, it's all right. Thank you for your concern.'

OBIT 5

With scuttled thoughts and inspirations,
With jettisoned elaborations,
The deepening Suez of his brain
Grew blocked and silted up again.

At Oxford men with spiked sticks shamble doggedly along between the tracks impaling litter – some of it most unsavoury – which they transfer into large wicker fruit-baskets carried in their free hand. Elsewhere the train often slows to a crawl to pass gangs of labourers engaged in replacing sleepers or raking ballast with long-tined forks out of Dante. Porters in shabby uniforms, some of them middle-aged and looking far from robust, carry huge loads, while other station staff do various kinds of hard manual work. These men and their activities would not be out of place in a film of *Anna Karenina*.

Meanwhile, computers control (?) the signalling system, and so-called High Speed Trains roar to and fro using two engines to reach speeds attained years before by Mallard and the Flying Scotsman. Millions of pounds have also been spent on developing something else called the A.P.T. which stands for Advanced Passenger Train. (cf. calling a pub the New Inn.) Anachronistic Passenger Train would be more apt.

'They' have the technology, 'They' have the capability to alleviate conditions for staff and passengers alike. Ours not to reason why 'They' prefer to squander their knowledge and their money on grandiose schemes which have nothing to do with human beings.

Paddington Station. Along the route stations are anxious to declare their identity. Strings of signs on lamp-posts tell us: Reading, Reading, Reading; Maidenhead, Maidenhead, Maidenhead, Maidenhead; Slough, Slough, Slough, Slough, Slough. But here you can with difficulty find any indication that you have arrived at Paddington, and no indication whatsoever that you have reached London. As a child I was never easily persuaded that this was my destination and I ought to alight. You are simply expected to know, just as football commentators expect you to know that Anfield means Liverpool, Molyneux Wolverhampton, The Dell Southampton, Gay Meadow Shrewsbury, and so on.

Once you have accepted the enormous secret of Paddington, you can appreciate its charms. The high echoing fane of the train-shed, where flit and perch pigeons and pied wagtails, has been repainted and vies with King's College Chapel in its blend of engineering achievement and graceful airiness. The ranks of pews where strangers and pilgrims used to be able to sit and commune, if not with God, at least with the shade of Isambard Kingdom Brunel, have gone. The weakest go to the wall now – or to Platform 1.

Paddington possesses some fourteen platforms, yet Platform 1 has a virtual monopoly of facilities. Fortune favours Oxford passengers, as our trains often depart from Platform 1. This means that in mild weather we can relish the odd sensation of taking refreshment under coloured umbrellas, doubly canopied by the station roof. Being indoors yet outdoors at the same time we feel like extras in a film studio, while the trains add a further element of surreality.

Paddington can be enjoyed by most people. Didcot, however, is a station for connoisseurs. Presumably the money ran out before 'They' could give Didcot the Oxford treatment, so they have just repainted all the old woodwork and left it at that. The result is elegant, restrained, yet perfectly functional.

One of the few genuine pleasures which commuting affords is to alight at Didcot on a spring or summer evening, to stroll to the end of the long platform (you may well send rabbits scuttling for cover round the boles of the young horse chestnuts), to gaze for a few moments at the placid fields and hills (carefully keeping your back to the dreary town of Didcot), then, turning, slowly to approach the long curves of the wooden canopies which, with their drooping jagged points, look like gravid fruit trees invented by Edward Lear, or pterodactyls with heraldically outstretched wings.

Scarcely ever write (or even read) my fair copy on the train, unless alone in a compartment or drunk – two similar states, for solitude intoxicates. I scribble in smaller ringbacked notebook what Lawrence Durrell calls work-points, to be expanded or modified later. Difficult to decide what to note. Laziness makes a good editor. Process like trying not to vomit. When I can resist no longer, struggle to get out notebook is like race against time to grab a paper bag. Commuting makes me train-sick. Result: these gobbets.

So many negative notices on the train. Should like to rephrase some of them. 'If a cool draught is desired please open windows beyond arrows.' 'Please feel free to use the lavatory while the train is in motion.' 'Alarm signal – proper use can save lives.' 'Lean out of the window for decapitation.' The positive approach. Sadly the chivalrous 'Gentlemen lift the seat', with its antithesis 'Ladies lower the seat', no longer applies. Modern seats do not remain upright, and those who lift them risk serious injury.

MYSTERY 5

Plaintive pleas over the Paddington tannoy for a mythical figure whom R. has dubbed 'the upside-down trolley-driver'. He seems to be invoked in times of crisis. The railwaymen's god. No one has ever beheld him. One apocalyptic day he will reveal himself as a kind of inverted Juggernaut on a great Weltrol hauled by fire-breathing locomotives, on to whose wheels the faithful, high on diesel fumes, will rush to immolate themselves.

A few of the professions regularly represented on the train:

clergyman	doctor	lawyer
accountant	civil servant	stamp auctioneer
chartered surveyor	wine merchant	copy-writer
publisher	designer	estate agent
management consultant	mathematician	nutritionist
editor	cartoonist	broadcaster
welfare officer	soldier	airman
market researcher	civil engineer	caterer
architect	English teacher	underwriter
economist	exporter	beautician
cartographer	lexicographer	theatrical agent
nurse	MP	photographer

also a helicopter salesman, a specialist in remote sensing and satellite imagery, a genetic engineer, a tropical agriculturalist, an ichthyologist, and even a psychiatrist. NB: not a single manual worker or artisan. The damned. All human death is here.

ANTI-KONTAKION 4

A curse on the train. Subverter of notions. Freezer of emotions. Wrecker of concepts. Mocker of precepts. Changer of gold into dross. Turner of profit to loss. Stander of theories on their head. Sender of dust and ashes instead. Anathema sit.

TRAIN GAMES 2 AND 3

Ran into A. who used to be a regular member of our group during my first year. 'How's the commuting?' he inquired, and added: 'I miss the intellectual cut and thrust.'

You can wax nostalgic even about commuting. I remember those early, palmy days when up to a dozen of us used to meet on the 1815. We occasionally indulged in something worthy of the name of conversation. But more often the intellectual cut and thrust was provided by The Times *quiz, when A. and I would take it in turns to test each other on the contents of the morning newspaper. Or we would play Napoleon, a variant of Twenty Questions introduced by*

R. (I had them all stumped the day I decided to be Archbishop Makarios.)

Both of these pastimes could provoke great hilarity and sometimes caused us to be viewed askance by staider travellers. Childish, perhaps, but there was a je ne sais quoi, a carefreeness about those days. We would arrive at Oxford completely relaxed, each ready to assume his home *persona*. Ubi sunt? Woriath tha winsalo. *Rust corrodes the buffet-car. The more mature and responsible the commuter, the more diminished and dehumanised the man.*

MYSTERY 6

Spotted more than once on platform at Oxford, a small pile of cardboard boxes each bearing legend:

> The 'crumpet' that leaves the desire for more.

If the boxes contained the kind of crumpets that you eat, the inverted commas would be otiose. Can only suppose, therefore, that the boxes – not large enough to accommodate animate 'crumpet' – must conceal some form of pornography.

Trains frequently stop. An alert commuter needs but a glance to ascertain his whereabouts on these occasions. (Alert commuter, however, a virtual contradiction in terms.) At one time or another the train will have halted at practically every point on the line. While others fret, a canny commuter takes advantage of hold-ups carefully to study his surroundings, memorising distinctive features for future reference. Not only does such topographical knowledge reassure, it can also have greater value in times of crisis when we need to weigh the pros and cons of whether to get out and walk or to stay aboard and sweat it out.

By day, we should know what we see. By night, we must *interpret* what we see, ambushing meanings like Tennyson's Tiresias. With experience we should be able to crack the coded message of a single light glimpsed through a steamed-up pane.

But we must not be fooled into thinking that the development of minor accomplishments such as this will help us in the long run to survive. Perhaps the wisest commuters are, after all, those who see nothing, learn nothing, know nothing. They have no delusions. They resemble those sailors who refuse to master the art of swimming so that they may drown quickly and painlessly if their ship sinks. Palinurus sought to escape death by swimming ashore, but when he landed the natives murdered him. True survival only begins when commuting ends.

TRAIN GAME 4

Counting birds. Between Oxford and Paddington, on any daylight journey, you can see about twenty varieties: e.g. rook, crow, wood pigeon, mallard, mute swan, moorhen, starling, house sparrow, heron, coot, pheasant, lapwing, magpie, black-headed gull, kestrel, blackbird, thrush, partridge, pied wagtail, Canada goose. With ornithological knowledge, reasonable eyesight, and luck – such as an unscheduled halt in a promising habitat (the Adlestrop factor) – you may add to that list various smaller birds, hard to spot at speed: skylark, linnet, chaffinch, yellowhammer, corn bunting, robin, and so on; as well as migrants such as swift, swallow, cuckoo and warblers; together with more unusual birds like lesser spotted, greater spotted and green woodpeckers, great crested grebe, tufted duck, redshank, snipe etc. Note the preponderance of water-loving birds which emphasises the damp and marshy nature of our route.

But this bird-counting proves nothing. It recalls a childhood spent in pleasant places learning to identify the birds. To what purpose? Now it serves as just another futile way of passing the futile journey.

Must confess myself superstitious to extent of saying: If I see ten different kinds of bird between Didcot and Oxford this evening, I shall consider that lucky. Between five and ten will be neither lucky nor unlucky. Less than five will be distinctly inauspicious. (Auspex = one who observes the flight of birds, to take omens thence. Tiresias excelled in this art.)

To such pathetic private ploys am I, and doubtless other commuters (megalomania begins in believing oneself unique), reduced by the tyrannical train.

> Had we but world enough, and time,
> Commuting daily were no crime.

Constant commuting affects our sense of perspective. We see everything in terms of the train, in relation to the train. We get our train legs and feel disoriented and dizzy off the train, lurching like freshly disembarked sailors. When the train approaches the platform where we wait, metaphysically we are already aboard. Bilocation comes naturally to us. The actual transfer of our bodies a trivial formality. We find the subtle shift which occurs when we alight (especially when for the first time we stand still in a setting we have always whizzed through) a mind-blowing, mystical experience.

OBIT 6

A coffin by the railway
Stirred him to ask: 'How far away,
How many stations up the line,
Awaits the one predestined mine?'

Architectural peculiarities at Paddington evoke monasteries on Mount Athos. Quaint balconied bow-windows, eccentric iron and plaster work, imposing doorcases would seem less out of place on the Holy Mountain in some vast decaying Russian skete, inhabited by two or three senile monks, than they do here.

It would be fun to commission Mr Felix Kelly to paint Paddington *qua* monastery, with bearded porters in stovepipe hats and rusty black cassocks loading luggage on to donkeys; the whole thing transplanted to some craggy site overlooking the Aegean. In the proper tradition of patrons I would ask him to depict me inconspicuously in a corner, telling my beads in the sun with not a train in sight.

At Paddington, as with some of the more run-down Athonite communities, you know that what lies behind the elaborate façade is not what originally lay behind it, not what was intended to lie behind it. This feeling, I think, rather than a perception of superficial resemblance, first caused the analogy to enter my mind – an intuition of ornate exterior, as two-dimensional as stage scenery, fronting dust, bare floorboards, crumbling plaster, peeling paper, mice, decay. For 'Ozymandias' read 'Isambard Kingdom Brunel'.

Announcements over loudspeaker systems play a large part in commuters' lives. First we have to train our ears to unscramble the garbled sounds. Next we discover, by trial and error, which parts of the station have the best acoustics. Then we have to interpret what we hear. We soon learn not to disregard anything. A seemingly innocuous message – 'Will a shunter go to the Bristol end of Platform 1' can spell trouble and delay to the epopts. When we catch that the coaches for a Cardiff or Swindon train have been delayed by 'operating difficulties in the carriage sidings', we do not jump for joy, for we recognise a knell that also tolls for us. But I must confess to succumbing to a certain smug satisfaction when I heard that the new million-pound push-me-pull-you had been delayed by 'locomotive failure'. Most commuters have a streak not only of masochism, but also of Providence-tempting *Schadenfreude*.

To be seen just outside Paddington, tucked in beside the tracks: a small brick building with a chimney, reminiscent of the wolf-resistant cottage constructed by the prudent pig. Over the door in bold coloured letters: UNCLE TOM'S CABIN. A wendy-house for railwaymen.

MYSTERY 7

Towards the western end of Paddington's Platform 1, a staircase leads down to a door which a notice declares to be an entrance to 'Paddington (Passengers) Dining Club'. Have never seen anyone enter or leave. How do you become a member? A discreet tap on the shoulder as you wait for the 1815? A cryptic summons over the tannoy? A message delivered on a silver salver as you speed towards Oxford? Then an interview with the SM and his ASMs. 'Congratulations! Over a long period we have observed you to be a most exemplary passenger ... We have pleasure in admitting you to membership of the Dining Club.' Lastly, there must be some kind of induction ceremony, an awe-inspiring ritual, never to be divulged, whose nature I had better not even guess at lest, stumbling upon the truth, I incur some Olympian penalty such as being chained to a Conflat and dragged perpetually to and fro through the gauntlet of the sprays and rotating brushes of the Britannia train-cleansing system. A Palinuran fate.

A railway proverb: A key in the door indicates an empty locker.

Have yet to discover either the official name or the rude porters' grosser name for those yellow electric 'donkeys' which, at Paddington, tend to try either to mow you down unawares by nipping along a platform beside an arriving train, or to make you miss your departing train by towing very slowly across the concourse an impenetrable wall of about two dozen luggage trolleys.

Do not know whether each 'donkey' works to one loco-motive. Some of them have names like Western Gauntlet or Western Renown roughly lettered on their battle-scarred sides. But this may simply declare a driver's admiration for a particular engine. At least one of them has, crudely drawn underneath the word KILLED, a macabre tally of ten or so matchstick men. It may not be a joke.

Unequivocal notice above a doorway on Reading Station:

Strictly Private
NO PUBLIC ADMITTANCE.

Sheep	**Goats**
1. Queue in orderly British fashion for trains at Paddington even when not specifically instructed to do so.	Never queue, especially when asked to do so. Wait in bar and approach train from far, unfrequented, end of platform.
2. Never attempt to tinker with heating, lighting or ventilation in carriage or compartment.	Learn location and function of knobs and switches. Always adjust these and windows to suit individual preferences. Never consult wishes of sheep.
3. Huddle together in a flock on platform. Seldom stray.	Never form flocks. Avoid sheep by fanning out on platform. Always prepared to walk long distances.

Sheep	**Goats**
4. Board nearest coach and stay put. Would rather stand than leave security of flock to search for seats. Too timorous to insinuate themselves into 8-seat compartments already containing 6 or 7 people.	Enjoy exploring train. Believe security lies in independence. Revel in individual initiative. Only stand in crises when most sheep get left behind. Happily occupy last seat in a compartment, moving, if necessary, luggage, animals or babies. Impervious to comments and black looks.
5. Cannot orientate themselves on train. Extreme cases are uncertain which end locomotive is, even when train in motion.	Intuitively know the length of a train and their own position aboard it. Can find the buffet-car blindfold.
6. Never think ahead. Seldom think at all. E.g. will put ticket in cardigan pocket, put cardigan in hold-all, put hold-all on rack, put overcoat on top of hold-all; agitated by arrival of ticket-inspector, forget where ticket is, spend hours searching, perhaps fruitlessly.	Always think ahead, often subconsciously. Like good footballers have wide peripheral vision and instinctively take up strategic positions. Win themselves time and space. Agile, but never waste effort.
7. Do not see or hear. Blind mouths that scarce know how to hold a shunter's hook. Tend to mistake Didcot – Reading even – for Oxford.	Always listen to announcements and read notices. Constantly alert. Know the terrain.
8. Have too much luggage.	Travel light.

9. Goats leap around, reconnoitre, butt, kick, complain, get into arguments, break regulations. Mr Francis Dodgson, who halted a boat train in Essex, on 5 March 1975, when his own commuter train had failed to arrive, by standing on the track, is clearly a hircine paragon. British Rail took him to court and a spokesman said: 'The man's actions were nothing short of lunacy.' (The boat train was travelling at 15 mph at the time.) But commuters everywhere hail Dodgson as a hero.

Sheep, on the other hand, accept their lot and safely graze, bleating blankly while goats are cast out with wailing and gnashing of briefcases. As usual, Jesus knew what he was talking about – in the end sheep always win.

Have been dipping again into *The Unquiet Grave* by Palinurus. Have always felt great empathy with it. Now it
assumes new significance for me. A contrived, premeditated
notebook on a single, or related, theme(s). Palinurus floated
up from my subconscious to present himself as a prototype,
a rival even, a promising enemy. Reopened the book to light
almost at once upon this:

Angoisse des Gares: A particularly violent form of Angst. . . . un-
bearable when arriving in London, if only from a day in Brighton
. . . Sensations worse at arriving in the evening than the morning,
and much worse at Victoria and Waterloo than at Paddington.
. . . much of our anxiety is caused by the horror of London itself
. . . Angst begins at Reading (for Paddington) . . . First-class or
third makes no difference. 'They' will get you, Palinurus, 'they'
aren't taken in.

He apparently never commuted, and therefore erred in
identifying the cause of the angst as horror of London. No,
Palinurus, the train itself was what brought on the anxiety
in one as sensitive as yourself. You must have felt the
countless unexpiated souls of commuters supplicating for
vengeance. But that is incidental. Was delighted, anyway,
to rediscover that our lines, if they do not actually cross, at
least touch. *Sortes Palinuranae*. An encouraging omen.

LITERARY LANDMARK 2, NUNEHAM HOUSE

*Visible between Radley and Culham. William Whitehead, an
eighteenth-century Poet Laureate, used to stay here. When Lord
Harcourt high-handedly shifted the village from beside the big house
to its present site, one woman, Barbara Wyatt, refused to budge from
her home. This early example of a sit-in proved successful and she was
allowed to remain. William Whitehead (taking care not to criticise
Lord Harcourt) wrote two poems about the episode:*

> To her no greater bliss could be
> Than in her cottage still to live
> And die beside her fav'rite tree . . .

She would not be moved. Nor should we.

Remember how, as a boy, I used to trespass on the railway. Used to try to walk along the track treading only on the sleepers, which were not ideally spaced for childish strides. Sometimes would miss my footing. Writing this Notebook I have a sense of proceeding in the same delicate manner from sleeper to sleeper. Must avoid the shifting, sharp, ankle-twisting ballast of commuters' stereotyped grievances, or hoary criticisms of British Rail. That is not what I meant at all. That is not it, at all.

> I walked in Hellas years ago
> With friends in white attire:
> And I remember how my soul
> Drank wine as pure as fire.
> (James Elroy Flecker)

The sixty-mile strip of landscape offered to us each day frequently stirs Grecian memories. Sometimes between Didcot and Cholsey can scarcely believe we are not passing through Boeotia. Plataea nestles at the foot of the Kithaeron Downs. Wheat covers the undulating Theban plain. The Asopos seems strangely swollen, but still smells the same as it flows between rushes and willows. We go too fast to see the little wild red tulips.

Nearer London we might be approaching Athens from Eleusis, through Aigaleo, by the profaned Sacred Way with its light industry, scrapyards, vacant lots and tall blocks of flats. I do not necessarily prefer the rural to the urban scene. Why should not Langley hold mysteries? Both allure me. Both arouse Greek longings. Both urge: Leave for Cape Sounion tonight!

The Thames accompanies us. We cross it again and again. A diagram of our route might look like a linked column of dollar signs on their sides: ⎓⎓⎓⎓ . The iron road: straight, economical, business-like. The waterway: meandering, lavish with space, unhurried. The river reproaches us. 'Quick bright things come to confusion,' it warns. It particularly reproaches me who have read William Morris's *News from Nowhere*. The permanent way –

what a presumptuous name! Or is it a hopefully apotropaic term analogous to the hostile Euxine or vengeful Eumenides, or the hideous kind of euthanasia experienced by commuters? In Morris's utopian, twenty-first-century England the railway has vanished. His characters row idyllically from Hammersmith to Kelmscott – characters who have no conception of or use for education, machinery, commerce, politics, or working for money, let alone commuting. They see transformed some of the places we sway or lurch through daily:

. . . we were soon going up the once sorely becockneyed reaches of the river about Maidenhead, which now looked as pleasant and enjoyable as the up-river reaches.

I should like to have seen with my own eyes what success the new order of things had had in getting rid of the sprawling mess with which commercialism had littered the banks of the wide stream about Reading and Caversham: certainly everything smelt too deliciously in the early night for there to be any of the old careless sordidness of so-called manufacture.

The railway having disappeared, and therewith the various level bridges over the streams of Thames, we were soon through Medley Lock . . .

How bitterly ironic that Oxford, comparatively unscathed in the 1890s, should subsequently have had imposed upon it the sordidness of so-called manufacture by another William Morris! The worst epithet the author of *News from Nowhere* could find for the city was 'don-beridden'.

Yes, the river reproaches us and we heed it not. We seldom see a skiff or other rowing-boat. Some of our own number attempt to escape for a week or so by hiring floating motor cars and driving up and down the Thames. If the river reproaches us, it scorns them. Escape does not lie that way. Escape lies in complete renunciation of commuterdom, of commuter time, speed, and mode of progression for those of the river.

I do not mean that we should all literally adopt a potamic way of life, though I know of at least one commuter who has become a contented lock-keeper. Having learnt that the shortest distance between two points is a straight line, man rashly assumes that he will gain something by taking such a route. If necessary, he tunnels, bridges, cuts, embanks and bores to realise this delusory ideal. But life-lines curve, are flexible. A straight line is a death-line. Every day the river offers us a life-line, a rippling clue of thread. We have only to grasp it to find our way out of the labyrinth and elude the Minotrain for ever. Every day that we reject the proffered thread brings inexorably nearer our turn to furnish the monster with his regular tribute of broken bodies and spirits.

ANTI-KONTAKION 5

A curse on the train. Betrayer of truth. Destroyer of youth. Padded cell whose inmates prefer to remain. Lumbering, ground-bound aeroplane. That which no commuter claims for a friend. That which claims every commuter in the end. Anathema sit.

Sometimes we halt looking into the depths of a copse or wooded cutting. Silence falls. Perhaps a wren trills. A cool odour, compounded of moss, leaf-mould, sap, vegetation, drifts into the carriage. I will the train to move on. It hurts to recall how once I walked in woods, once understood undergrowth. The laurel trees still stand, *mais moi, je n'y vais plus.*

OBIT 7

A magpie glimpsed among sparse trees
Gave premonition of disease.

Winter. Early morning. A man with a tractor and trailer drops hay-bales for steam-exhaling cattle in a frosty field. Les trop pauvres heures de M. Vert.

We see few human beings in fields or streets. On some days the world might have ended. No peasants populate the landscape. The farmers sit snug in their offices. Buildings or vehicles encapsulate everyone, except for a golfer or two, a lone sculler, a man shooting pigeons, children at play, and a handful of other moderately sane beings. We never pause to question this state of affairs. How did it arise? Did we choose it? Do we like it? Could we change it? Should we try to change it? Dangerous questions!

Do railwaymen have a particular church to which they repair to give thanks for safe journeys? Where they can hear railway sermons worthy to stand beside the whaling sermon in *Moby Dick*? Where marble locomotives surmount their memorials when they have been shunted away to the happy marshalling-yards beyond the terminal buffers?

Ticket-collectors or inspectors. World-weary figures who have seen it all. Each has his own distinctive gimmick or gambit. One flings open the door with a crash, shouting: 'You are requested for your rail tickets please.' Another sneaks up silently and waits patiently for people to become aware of his presence. Most behave gently towards sleepers, but one, with curling mustachios, delights in rapping the table very sharply with his ticket-punch in order to terrify dozers into wakefulness.

We soon become familiar with the regulars: the one who peers severely over his half-moon spectacles; the one with the falsetto voice who squeaks: 'Thank you, sir' or 'Thank you, madam' to every single passenger; the keen young one whose hat is too big; the lugubrious one with the Cyrano de Bergerac conk. But one, strangely, I only encountered once, and have not found another commuter who knows of him. He inspected the tickets exclaiming alternately as he went: 'Lovely grub!' 'Sweet music!' 'Lovely grub!' 'Sweet music!' Such an approach might pall repeated day after day, but experienced just the once it had a certain charm and aroused curiosity. Perhaps he was doing it for a bet.

Reading General. 0800. Drama. Train is moving off when a girl's shrill voice blasts us out of our matutinal coma. Desperate. Near to hysterics. 'Stop the train,' she screams, 'there's someone coming!' 'Shut that door!' commands a porter. 'No, NO!' she yells, as if being raped. A few tense seconds later her husband – they look like a honeymoon couple – who had ill-advisedly alighted to buy coffee, appears calmly from the next coach. He has reboarded the train further down and walked along the corridor. He soothes his young wife. Their marriage may survive, but our peace has been irrecoverably shattered. 'Hmm,' grunts the middle-aged commuter next to me, 'this train gets more like the Orient Express every day.'

Can't find any reference to trains or commuting in Cyril Connolly's *Enemies of Promise* (1938). Yet commuting is an arch-enemy of promise. Perhaps it has only really become so in the last thirty years with the broadening of the commuter belt, of London's magnetic field. Commuting destroys more souls than any of the hazards Connolly explores. For, however corrupting your job, however much it tends to divert you from your creative purpose, if you live within fifteen minutes of it, you still have a chance of working out your own salvation in your spare time, of making your soul. But if you spend four hours travelling every day, you are as good as lost, whatever your occupation. The longer you remain in this purgatory, the more likely you are to slip into the easy descent to Avernus.

If only 'They' would close Oxford Station, thus making the decision for me. A feeble *cri de gare*!

In our commuting heyday, over a period of a year or so, we held farewell parties on the train for J., A., B., and N. It was J., in publishing, who established the precedent that black velvet – Guinness and champagne – was obligatory on these occasions. A marvellous, treacherous drink, it slides down the gullet very easily and, if you start drinking at Paddington, hits you around Didcot. One of the few skills I acquired at university is a fatal facility for opening champagne bottles with minimum palaver. This means that mine is the glass which catches the overflow, and thus I grow inebriated more quickly than those around me. Anyway, that's my excuse for having arrived at Oxford, after at least two of those parties, in a state of utterly irresponsible euphoria. Once I ended up in a field, in the middle of the night, with my arms around the neck of a donkey.

Once upon a time . . . With the connivance of the

buffet-car staff we would commandeer three or four tables and set to. Self-consciousness and awareness of other passengers soon passed as kef was generated. No need to describe the growing conviction of brilliance which accompanied such gatherings, especially when spiced with the added ingredient of motion. Ah! We fondly believed that thus we could beat the system. That by cocking several snooks at commuting we proved ourselves a superior breed to those who trundle daily to and from points south of the Thames. Fools! The only winners were those to whom we were bidding farewell. Unimpressed, impervious, the train, like the Oxus river at the end of *Sohrab and Rustum*, floated on.

MYSTERY 8

Europe's Largest Mechanised Depot For Domestic Fuel, declares a vast sign at West Drayton. This notice, probably one of the largest hoardings in Europe, partially hides what appears to be a charmingly small coalyard. It provokes speculation. Why has this gigantic board been placed where train passengers can read it? Why, indeed, has it been erected at all? If the information is true, we can only marvel a) that in the whole of Europe there exists no larger mechanised depot for domestic fuel than this modest triangle; and b) that presumably someone – a team perhaps – must have travelled the length and breadth of Europe, seeking out and measuring depots for domestic fuel (while rejecting mechanised depots for industrial fuel, and unmechanised depots for domestic fuel such as the great peasant woodpiles of eastern Europe), to ensure that the boast were no idle one. Did the researchers also tour other continents to discover, to their chagrin, larger mechanised depots in America or Asia which precluded a claim for global supremacy? How are we, mere passers-by, to benefit from the fruit of their investigations? Could the whole thing constitute a subtle exercise in Common Market propaganda? While straining at the gnat of the largest mechanised depot for domestic fuel, we unsuspectingly swallow the camel of a begged question which places West Drayton firmly on the map of Europe.

Talking of depots or *dépôts*, a large shed at Reading used to have, in tall, individually supported letters along its roof-ridge, the words GOODS DEPÔT. Somebody had risked life and limb to attach that circumflex. Who knows, perhaps he fell still clutching the acute accent for the E? Today those letters have been removed, while to the (safer) side of the building has been affixed a sign describing the place as an unaccentuated DEPOT. What price Europe now?

Slap beside the West Drayton depot squats a minute wooden shack scarcely robust enough to support the signboard nailed to it, which reads: Temporary Coal Office. It must surely be Europe's smallest . . .

The Reverend W. Awdry, author of books for children about railway engines with names like Thomas, Henry and James, has a down on trucks. He casts them as the villains of his stories, as malicious, obstinate, stupid delinquents. The virtuous engines always triumph in the end, even if it means smashing a recalcitrant truck into matchwood. I do not know or inquire why a Christian priest should offer young readers the unchristian ethic that all trucks are intrinsically wicked and in need of violent correction, even annihilation. But, religion apart, I consider him unfair to trucks. Since, in an idle moment on the train, I began truck-spotting, I have been discovering their appeal, their fascinating variety, their names, their shapes, their functions. *O nobile themis trux!* I have developed an affection for them. Prawn and Grampus, Lowmac and Palvan, Ash and Banana, truculently will I support you against the Reverend Awdry and Thomas and the other engines. Keep on trucking!

In his inaugural lecture as Professor of Poetry at Oxford, W.H. Auden gave 'four questions which, could I examine a critic, I should ask him'. He said: 'If a critic could truthfully answer "yes" to all four, then I should trust his judgement implicitly on all literary matters.' The first (I will not bother here with the other three) was: 'Do you like, and by like I really mean like, not approve of on principle, long lists of proper names such as the Old Testament genealogies or the Catalogue of Ships in the *Iliad*?'

I do not place great value on Auden's *imprimatur*, but it pleases me to know that I share with someone of his calibre a liking for lists of ships, trucks, words, birds, professions or whatever, and also to be reminded that the precedents go back to Homer and the Bible. Short catalogues – not the whole of the telephone directory or *Who's Who* – have a magic, incantatory quality amounting to much more than the simple sum of their parts.

OBIT 8

He never said: 'I am not well',
But lived withdrawn. So thin the shell
Between the brain and heart, so brittle;
He thought too much and felt too little.

Here, then, another list – of some of the landmarks and sights along our daily route: the towers, spires and multi-storey car-park of Oxford; Boar's Hill; Nuneham House; Didcot power station; Wittenham Clumps; the Chiltern Hills; the Berkshire Downs; Basildon House; Goring Gap; again and again the Thames; Reading Gaol; Sutton's seed trial grounds; Windsor Castle; Heathrow jets; Wormwood Scrubs . . .

Beautiful sights, interesting sights, but never ours to possess, to experience. No sooner glimpsed than snatched away. Mocking visions of a land promised to another tribe than ours, the unchosen ones. A land where even a stretch in prison offers more satisfaction than this zombie half-life.

Auden again, in the Foreword to *The Dyer's Hand*: 'In going over my critical pieces, I have reduced them, when possible, to sets of notes because, as a reader, I prefer a critic's notebooks to his treatises.'

Should like to discover more about this genre, not chosen by me but imposed upon me. A late-twentieth-century commuter who wants to write something creative surely has no alternative to some kind of notebook with an overall theme or themes. A disjointed medium for a disjointed existence. Deliberate but not planned. A preconceived expedition without a predetermined route.

Have not read widely enough to know much about antecedents. Most printed notebooks have not been produced with an eye to publication, and have appeared posthumously. They tend to be ragbags containing the trimmings and cabbage from a lifetime's output of suits and dresses, plus materials and patterns for other garments never sewn. When Auden says he prefers 'a critic's notebooks', he means this kind of random by-product rather than his own contrived efforts. He seems to think that both belong to the same genre. I doubt it.

Very few works fall into the category of the Premeditated Notebook. Auden cheated in *The Dyer's Hand* by working backwards from continuous prose. Anyway, instinct tells me that literary criticism is not a legitimate subject for the P.N. Elsewhere, however, Auden has produced fine examples, notably the Journal of an Airman in *The Orators* which, like Lawrence Durrell's *Prospero's Cell*, qualifies as a P.N. because the sketchy diary framework is so obviously an artifice.

Durrell's novels abound in fascinating extracts from hypothetical notebooks. He has also given us *The Red Limbo Lingo*, subtitled A Poetry Notebook. Alas, the notes occupy only fourteen pages. 'Alas', because in those pages he offers a tantalising brief indication of how a brilliant P.N. might be written on a single theme, in this case that of blood. Elliptic surrealism – that's the way to do it if you have it in you. Avoid plodding verbiage.

Oddly, Cyril Connolly (*Sunday Times* 5/9/71) missed the point of *The Red Limbo Lingo*, writing: 'his long introductory prose poem does not seem to me the most successful'. How could he fail to identify an incipient P.N. when, a quarter of a century previously, alias Palinurus, he had issued his own Premeditated Notebook *par excellence*? Did he leave his *alter ego* unburied on a wartime beach-head? Whatever the case, *The Unquiet Grave* remains a paragon and paradigm of the genre. The more I try to bring this poor sooterkin into the world, the more I appreciate Palinurus's achievement. If a thing is worth doing at all, it is worth doing badly; then at least you gain insight into the workings of better crafted exemplars.

Sequels to *The Unquiet Train*: *The Truck Pool*, *The Condemned*

Guard's Van, The Missing Conflats, Devious Connections, Les Pullmans, The Morning Cavalcade.

How hard to find or create a period of undisturbed time sufficient for the composition and setting down of even one thought-out paragraph. Cannot write on train because a) am too decrepit to control the pen, and b) when not asleep I find the distractions too demanding. How do writers of more sustained prose manage? By cutting out the ratiocination?

Our journey, like a good allegory, has many levels, offers many morals, invites anagogy.

And he said unto me, This miry slough is such a place as cannot be mended: it is the descent whither the scum and filth that attends conviction for sin doth continually run, and therefore it is called the Slough of Despond; for still as the sinner is awakened about his lost condition, there arise in his soul many fears and doubts, and discouraging apprehensions, which all of them get together, and settle in this place. And this is the reason of the badness of this ground.

What an exceedingly apposite *donnée*! For around despondent Slough more than anywhere, as the factories flow or creep past, do discouraging apprehensions assault and assail the commuter's soul, as he reflects upon his lost condition.

But, this obvious parallel apart, ours is in general a Bunyanesque progress. At least three large prisons, as well as several cemeteries and graveyards, ought to remind us daily of human frailty and the futility of what Richard Cobb has called 'the regular urban itineraries of a respectable occupation'. But we proceed as though blinkered, and behave more like Obstinate, Pliable and Mr Wordly Wiseman than like Christian.

Every landmark, literary or not, has a message. Within us lies the power to interpret or ignore, to determine whether we see mud or stars, whether we lug our bulging briefcases to the end of the line, or whether our burdens loose from off our shoulders and fall from off our backs, leaving us glad and lightsome with merry hearts.

ANTI-KONTAKION 6

A curse on the train. Market selling goods of little worth. Garden killing seeds in barren earth. Puddle-jumper. Torture-chamber. Anathema sit.

Oxford cemetery. Behind stands Pickford's Depository. Interesting juxtaposition – we cannot take it with us when we go. The train so often pauses here on run-in to the station. Hoary legend that permission to build railway here was only granted on condition that drivers stopped beside the graveyard as a mark of respect for the dead. If true, many drivers today tempt providence by disregarding the tradition. I know of passengers who superstitiously avert their gaze, as if a sight of what we all must come to would somehow contaminate them. I prefer the attitude of the Cyreneans, members of the Simon Community for down-and-outs which also borders the railway. They make snug dens in the bowels of box bushes, and sometimes can be seen taking their ease against tombstones, enjoying sun and cider among the thrushes and blackbirds which feed on the well-nourished worms.

Nor can the impassive train afford complacency. We also pass several scrapyards and automobile ghats, with their reminder that machines too have limited life-spans.

TRACKSIDE INDUSTRY 1

Mr Wall erected blind red brick arches fit to induce teichopsia; Sir Erich Pasold plastered his premises with monster ladybirds; Horlick's built a crenellated fortress; Huntley and Palmer took architectural hints from Reading Gaol; Scott's Emulsion set up a mighty mosaic of a Norwegian with a colossal cod; – all because convention then decreed that grandiose façades should cover mundane, if not dark satanic, interiors. Today the pretence has been abandoned in deference more to the dictates of economy than to a desire for honesty. Each new factory or warehouse resembles the next. The jaded eye of the commuter searches for relics of the self-confident eccentricity of the past, or contemporary signs that here and there individuals are still asserting themselves.

A megalithic group like Didcot power station soon palls. Once you have admired the sheer size of the constituent elements, appreciated the interplay between the male chimney-stack and the female cooling-towers, tried it out at sunrise, by moonlight, in mist, under storm-clouds, you have exhausted its possibilities.

More complicated structures continue to please. You can scrutinise the Reading and Southall gasworks day after day for years without unravelling all their piped intricacies. I find particular satisfaction too in certain large, rambling constructions which look as if they are made from Meccano. They have struts and gantries, sides plated with moth-eaten corrugated iron, conveyor belts, covered aerial passages, cogs and pulleys, not to mention devices for inverting railway trucks and emptying out their contents as if they were so many punnets full of blackberries. What precise function they perform, I cannot say. Nor do I wish for a tour of the works with a detailed explanation of the humdrum process. Suffice it that, seen through a train window, they give pleasure, perhaps for no better or worse reason than that they recall the improbable inventions of absent-minded professors in the comics of our childhood.

Testing time. J. casually remarked to me: 'I see some young man has been and published a book about commuting to Fenchurch Street. You know, what he sees through the window of the train every day and that sort of thing.' Now we shall see whether I can practise what I preached, saying: 'Let every commuter write a notebook . . . let him publish and be saved.' If this young man's book enjoys great success, I may find it hard to maintain such objective equanimity. But I feel I have half won the battle by preparing myself to meet the situation before it arose. I shall not read this new book until I consider my own completed, for fear of being influenced by it. One thing I know: from now on I shall experience an added tremor whenever, playing Monopoly, I land on Fenchurch Street Station.

Difficult to pass aesthetic judgement on what we see from the train. We are so conditioned that we accept unquestioningly the beauty of the Berkshire Downs, the Chilterns, Goring Gap and other examples of nature unadulterated. But where man and nature collaborate – cultivated land, gravel pits – or where man ousts nature completely – railway stations, factories, pylons, roads, gasometers, machinery – we hesitate, our instruments function erratically.

Claude Lévi-Strauss suggests that:

. . . the upheaval we observe in the case of Impressionism, when we compare it with previous art forms, can be seen once more in the case of Cubism, which undertakes to teach men to live on friendly terms not so much with restricted suburban landscapes . . . as with the products of human industry. The world in which twentieth-century man has to live no longer admits even of those relatively rustic spots dear to Sisley or Pissarro. It is a world completely invaded by culture and the products of culture, and so develops a form of painting which seeks its chief sources of inspiration in manufactured objects.

On some days I derive more enjoyment from the suburban and urban than from the rural sections of the journey. I like the few old tenements which remain near Paddington, with their multi-jointed, many-angled drainpipes, washing drying on ledges like a colony of seagulls dotted across a cliff-face, and general air of teeming life. I like the sight of willowherb, ragwort and evening primroses flourishing in neglected sidings. I like the poplar-fringed allotments near Maidenhead.

On such days I find the 'relatively rustic', not to mention the totally rural (both of which, *pace* Lévi-Strauss, still exist), unstimulating, not to say downright dull. The French pundit would have me believe myself conditioned by painters like Cézanne, Picasso, Léger and Klee 'to live on friendly terms' with the works of man seen through the carriage window. I, reckoning art to have no bearing on the matter, dispute this, albeit in clichés such as 'I know what I like', 'beauty is in the eye of the beholder', 'everything is beautiful in its own way', 'there is nothing either good or bad but thinking makes it so'. But then, clichés *are* Truth, Truth clichés – that is all we need to know.

When we have to wait at Reading General we sometimes see a curious sight. A woman in grey uniform leads a small cross-section of the human race into a hole in the platform. A few moments later they reappear on the opposite platform and vanish through an exit. All this is strange enough, but what makes it even more remarkable is the effect of the uniform on the woman. An absurd grey pillbox hat, old-fashioned, high-heeled shoes, what look like real seamed nylon stockings, and, in between, this sort of 1950s New Look grey suit, tight and tapering. The costume forces its wearer to proceed in a teetering manner, bottom protruding, bosom jutting, anserine neck extended. Behind straggles a string of bewildered goslings.

The explanation commonly given for this performance – that the grisette is taking passengers to a coach for Heathrow Airport – does not make sense, because Reading is many miles from the aerodrome. Anyone wanting to go there by a combination of train and bus would naturally alight at West Drayton.

I offer another interpretation of this phenomenon. The girls are leaders of lost souls, psychopomps who guide their flock of wandering shades – whither? The ludicrous uniform signals that we should not take seriously the curious pageant. We must look for antecedents not in the tragedians, but in Aristophanes. The comic procession can only have one destination – a desirable, mythical cloud-cuckoo-land.

OVERHEARD 4

American, looking out of window near Oxford Station: 'Say, is that creek the Thames?'

People who live near the railway become oblivious of it. Houses generally face roads. The inmates devote time and attention to ensuring that they are not overlooked by passers-by. They often abandon their front gardens, front doors and front rooms altogether, scuttling round to the back parts of their houses where they feel more secure. But they ignore the trains.

Perhaps if they faced the railway they would reverse the

process. As it is, they blithely offer passengers, by day, the sight of their washing-lines weighed down with unmentionables, their rotting compost, their junk including souvenirs filched from the railway, unkempt cabbage-beds, and illegal caravans; by night, intimate glimpses, through lighted, uncurtained windows, of domestic scenes against a background of flickering television sets and posters of Great Uncle Bulgaria.

The train furnishes an ideal mobile hide for the commuter turned suburban anthropologist.

OBIT 9

Each year he would be more aware
When nature passed from clothed to bare,
Each year with less surprise remember
Some leaves stay green until November.

Railways are a form of communication. A book is a form of communication. Therefore this Notebook is a railway system. Not such a false syllogism as first appears. The form shapes itself to the subject, becomes the subject. I, the writer, am the Regional Controller. Words my rolling-stock. Nouns are trucks, adjectives coaches, verbs locomotives. I assemble train sentences. Container trains, passenger trains, milk trains, goods trains, mail trains, Pullmans, expresses, sleepers, stoppers, specials – inexhaustible types and combinations. I shunt and marshal the words. I manipulate the sentences. Dispatch them in phased flights to form paragraphs.

I make announcements: 'The next sentence has been cancelled due to verb failure. We regret the incoherence this will cause.' 'We apologise for the shortage of adjectives which is due to syntactical difficulties in the language sidings.' 'Will a grammarian please go to the London end of paragraph 118.' 'A message is conveyed by this train.' I am omnipotent but not, alas, infallible. Such a complex system can easily degenerate into chaos. As Controller I have to see that points and signals are set, stations prepared for the approach of trains, detonators placed when fog descends, that everything is in the right place at the right time. If I fail in any department, disaster will ensue in the form of crashes, *non sequitur*, collisions, anacoluthon, uncouplings, catachresis, derailments, solecisms, breakdowns, gibberish. Injury, even death, may result, and I shall lose my job.

Quotations could swamp Notebook. When I contemplate The Train In Literature, I realise that the difficulty lies in finding a modern book which does not contain at least a passing reference to a train or, indeed, a reference to a passing train. I could not hope to select extracts systematically, even if I wished to – which I certainly do not, for a notebook is nothing if not unsystematic. I have no criterion, then, in choosing literary allusions. I simply offer whatever turns up in the sidings of my mind. An aleatory mode of procedure not unlike a railway journey.

TRACKSIDE INDUSTRY 2

The Creative Press (Reading) Ltd sounds promising. Do they print original material for perusal? Their windowless warehouse looks distinctly uncreative, but it just might contain a series of cork-lined cubicles where authors, nourished on inexhaustible madeleines, *conduct seminal research into the recovery of lost time.*

LITERARY LANDMARK 3, THE CHILTERNS

From the train we cannot see the White Horse above Uffington, so no pretext for admitting G.K. Chesterton's Ballad of the White Horse. *But one morning, after days of parching summer drought, as we approached Cholsey, I was looking out of the window on the opposite side to the Berkshire Downs, watching the threat (or promise) of rain build up, when there drifted into my head a half-remembered line from Chesterton's* A Ballade of the First Rain. *Happily, then, he qualifies for inclusion after all:*

> *O fields of England, cracked and dry and dun,*
> *O soul of England, sick of words, and wan! –*
> *The clouds grow dark; – the down-rush has begun,*
> *– It comes, it comes, as holy darkness can,*
> *Black as with banners, ban and arriere-ban;*
> *A falling laughter all the valley fills,*
> *Deep as God's thunder and the thirst of man:*
> *(A storm is coming on the Chiltern Hills.)*

A. reports that, travelling up late on the 0903, he encountered both 'the mistress' ('She has more of a cared-for air than many a legal wife', Betjeman) and the girl who once massaged him at Maidenhead. The later the train, the more decadent and sybaritic.

Windows frame – a fact so obvious that we forget it. Everything we see from the train we see through a rectangular window. The outside world flows past our gaze like a film in a series of frames. If the train stops we find ourselves looking through a kind of slide-viewer. This cinematographic effect gives us the illusion that we are beholding something two-dimensional, a four-edged picture, and not reality. (Has anyone exploited artistically the device of moving an audience at high speed past a succession of stills?) We project ourselves into the landscape just as we would project ourselves into a film, mentally but not physically. We imagine that we could find happiness if only we could live in that house, walk in those fields, sail in that boat, sit under those trees, drink in that pub. We fall victim to the advertising technique which shows you photographs to suggest that the purchase of a product will give you the entrée to a new life. We overlook the fact that we cannot step through the frame without taking with us our bunions, our haemorrhoids, and all the other psychosomatic ailments which beset commuters. Only by quitting for good the Odeon womb of the train can we enter into full possession of unframed reality.

Looked up Goring, Reading, Maidenhead, Slough in a dictionary of place-names, thinking the provenance of such suggestive names might prove interesting. Should have known better. Their derivations turn out to be plain dull. In future shall give full rein to speculation. Facts only stifle thought.

To travel hopefully is a better thing than to arrive (Stevenson). Yes, but never to travel at all is a better thing than to commute.

Battered old open truck with 'For Chief Engineer's Use

Only' on the side. Pleasant to imagine him riding along in it, probably wearing a Stephensonian stovepipe hat.

Container trains. An engine towing a string of large boxes – the crudest possible arrangement – such as a child plays with. Not even a guard's van. A solid, moving, characterless wall. No clue to the contents. No romance. Hard corners, uncompromising. A box from Spain between one from America and one from Japan, like new hotels in different capitals – indistinguishable, interchangeable, modern.

Doubtless the Organisation and Methods men would like to see passengers similarly crated and freighted. (Whatever happened to cattle-trucks?) But a coffin cannot contain life, cannot contain the human spirit. A million bullion trains could not buy the most debased and degraded commuter. Even commuters have souls. Save Our Souls makes nonsense. In the end, when the goods trains go to Badsville, our souls will save *us*.

ANTI-KONTAKION 7

A curse on the train. Archive of every sleeping form. Archetype of the creeping worm. Arch-enemy of those who refuse to conform. Anathema sit.

In Spanish *loco* means 'insane'. In parts of the United States grows the loco-weed. If horses and cattle eat it they contract loco-disease which affects the brain. Palinurus uses this in *The Unquiet Grave*. But he does not make the railway connection. Dictionary maintains that 'locomotion' has something to do with 'moving from place to place', without explaining how the dative or ablative *loco* can suggest motion. No, 'locomotion' obviously means 'insane movement', a surfeit of which gives commuters (who travel for loco motives) loco-disease. We know the cause. We know the cure. All we need is faith and courage. Good *deus loci*, deliver us.

Hospital ward analogy recalls some statements of Dictator George Papadopoulos. He likened himself to a surgeon operating on Greece, the sick patient, who, he said, would recover, but not before spending a period encased in restricting plaster. Some people really believed him. Others thought it expedient to believe him. Just so do we commuters exist under the dictatorship of the train. We believe, or make ourselves believe, a) that we need medical attention, and b) that the course of treatment we are undergoing is beneficial. In fact a power-crazy maniac has us in his clutches. He uses us for his evil experiments in train-surgery, then casts us spent aside. He knows he can afford to treat us as expendable. New passengers queue to take our places, unaware of our fate. No one heeds me when I cry: 'The dictator has no clothes on!'

Strangeness of a train journey from Oxford to Birmingham. Unnatural pull in unaccustomed direction. Centrifugal. A succession of smiling, shirt-sleeved men leaning out of sunny signal-boxes. Foray into a pristine past. Feel like a disoriented tourist with no points of reference – suffering from train-lag. An animal (*Commuterus Vulgaris Ferrovianus*, Prasinus – dangerous when roused, do not feed or provoke) reared in captivity, bewildered, frightened by freedom. Familiarity breeds content. Oh for a glimpse of Maidenhead!

From Anthony Trollope's *Autobiography*:

Railroads afforded me my means of conveyance, and I found that I passed in railway-carriages very many hours of my existence. Like others I used to read, – though Carlyle has since told me that a man when travelling should not read, but 'sit still and label his thoughts'. But if I intended to make a profitable business out of my writing, and, at the same time, to do my best for the Post Office, I must turn these hours to more account than I could do even by reading. I made for myself therefore a little tablet, and found after a few days' exercise that I could write as quickly in a railway-carriage as I could at my desk. I worked with a pencil, and what I wrote my wife copied afterwards. In this way was composed the greater part of *Barchester Towers* and of the novel which succeeded it, and much also of others subsequent to them. My only objection to the practice came from the appearance of literary ostentation, to which I felt myself to be subject when going to work before four or five fellow-passengers. But I got used to it. . .

Some might argue that Trollope's novels display the kind of dull cleverness that one could expect from a civil servant scribbling on a train. A researcher might do worse than seek out Trollope's railway allusions and metaphors, proving, perhaps, that Trollope simply described what he could see out of the train window as he wrote. Be all that as it may, I know of no other authenticated case of a commuting writer.

Certainly I do not qualify. These jottings represent locomotion recollected in immobility. Conceivably I might make a 'tablet' and learn to execute my painful scrawl under commuting conditions. I have not sufficient Victorian self-confidence to imagine that my fellow-passengers might accuse me of 'literary ostentation'. But two things still bother me. One is the question of secrecy. I own to an anxiety bordering on the neurotic lest someone should read any part of what I write before I consider the whole ready to be divulged. Knowing that I myself never lose an opportunity to squinny at any document exposed, however briefly, by another traveller, I fear subjection to similar treatment by others.

But my main objection to writing or reading much on the train is that one *misses* things. One does not buy a ticket for the theatre and read a book or write letters throughout the show. The train ticket costs more – all the more reason for not spurning the entertainment provided, which frequently surpasses that to be seen on the stage, let alone in-flight movies. Trollope betrays a blind spot by relating that he schooled himself to write on the train, and thus, by implication, neglected to observe his fellow-men, the passing landscape, or even his own thoughts. Here indeed may lie the clue as to why Trollope remains worthy, admirable, competent, professional, but not great.

OBIT 10

As most of those who smiled seemed mad,
He chose to be thought sane and sad,
So never went out on the binge
But spent his life upon the fringe.

The old work of giants – the mighty engineering feats of

Brunel and the rest. They believed themselves to be pioneers working for the glory of God, Britain, and Queen Victoria, opening up a way to the West. Little did they dream how posterity would abuse, would desecrate their labours. Hope they rest in peace somewhere unshaken by the vibrations as the drab trainloads of tired commuters shuttle to and fro.

Railway companies do not cater for the needs of the human spirit. Indeed they do not recognise its existence. By ignoring it they suppress it. Shades of the prison-house. Nothing banishes intimations of immortality more effectively than commuting.

Well-meaning people run missions to darkest Africa, missions to seamen, missions to factory-workers, missions to alcoholics, missions to their own parishes. No missionary of any creed has ever ventured into our desolate territory. Our lost world figures on no map, not even as *terra incognita*. When we board the train we virtually cease to exist. We desperately need commuter-priests or travelling gurus. An unknown tribe, we await discovery. But no one can find us because no one realises we are there. No one ministers to us. Our souls atrophy. Doubtless the railway company would prefer us totally inanimate.

Some ships have their own chaplains. Aboard those that do not the captains can at least marry and bury. Guards, ticket-collectors and engine-drivers have no such powers. (Curiously, the only department where the train follows maritime custom is the bar, which observes no licensing hours while under way, and charges prices fit to cover the overheads incurred when each consignment of liquor has to be rowed out in a small tender over tossing seas.)

They order, said I, this matter better in Greece. They provide shrines at stations where you can light a candle and say a prayer before setting off. Many travellers cross themselves as the train starts. Some carry ikons in their luggage. Even if you neglect these observances, you can rest assured that the driver will have ikons in his cab, as well, very likely, as a reserve of small change to be flung out at trackside chapels.

Where there is no vision the people perish. However rich our spiritual lives in Oxford or in London, on the secular train our souls are at risk, not from positive evil so much as from accidie, the negative sin of not taking a joyful interest in everything around us. We need someone to come over *from* Macedonia to help us, to teach us how to retrieve vision, how to *see*.

If we do not put up a struggle, we shall arrive at the point reached by the protagonist in Arthur Koestler's *Darkness at Noon* as his execution looms:

Why had not the Public Prosecutor asked him: 'Defendant Rubashov, what about the infinite?' He would not have been able to answer – and there, there lay the real source of his guilt . . . Could there be a greater?

Paradoxically, if we do fight to keep the human spirit alive as we commute, we shall find ourselves well on the way to effecting our permanent escape from the soulless train.

Who fills the role of Palinurus? Brunel, unable to rest until his work is put to a worthy use again? Commuting man, drifting without salvation, lost in the interstices of the timetable? Or Cyril Connolly himself, pitching in the tides of literary fashion, his thin masterpiece awaiting release from the fat bulk of his *oeuvre*?

The train, like the jungle, is neutral. Ay, very like the jungle. It has its own law too – survival of the least imaginative. The train can be used to bring lovers together (or to part them), to start an expedition to the Amazon or a pilgrimage to the Holy Land, or day after day to grind a man down. In its steaming compartments skulk old campaigners who refuse to accept that the war has ended. Veterans determined never to lay down their briefcases and emerge into the light of day. The train does not care. All who travel on it have free will. There is no pre-destination.

TRACKSIDE INDUSTRY 3
Ideal Casements. Nothing magic about them. They open uncharmed

on the foam of detergent-polluted Thames. Next door, a useful service for flaccid commuters – General Galvanizing.

Shall soon qualify for certificate from Big Chief I-Spy declaring me an Honorary Truck-Spotter Second Class. Not always easy to distinguish purely arbitrary names from those descriptive of function. Is a Hop simply a receptacle (cf. hopper), or do brewers use it specifically for the conveyance of that climbing perennial dioecious plant so necessary for good beer? Do Sturgeons carry caviar? Can you sleep on a Bolster? Does a Grampus puff? Do Tubes travel underground? Can you dine off a Plate? Whatever happens in Sleeping and Messing Vans? Do Iron Ore Tipplers suffer from hangovers? What songs do Mermaids sing? Such puzzling questions are not beyond all conjecture. Anyway, when the wind is westerly, I know a Ling from a Lamprey.

COMMUTER'S CALENDAR 1
1 April: Lambs Leaping. Lovers. Launches. Leafage. Les Lapins Lolloping. Larks.

Night after night a distinguished-looking man patrols the corridors, searching, searching. He scrutinises us all intently. His melancholy mien remains constant. He never pauses, never speaks, seldom sits down. Once I awoke to find him squeezed in beside me as I sprawled over enough space for two people – elsewhere he could have had more room. I imagine him looking for a lost son, refusing to abandon hope.

In my mind I pair this questing man with another whom I see in the mornings: big, middle-aged, face of a wily old pike. Don't know what it is about him, but he looks dead – a true zombie. He radiates deadness as he lumbers up the aisle in his heavy overcoat.

Maybe I have died too, without realising. Men know that they are dying. How do they know afterwards that they have died? (*The Third Policeman.*) Why this is Hell, nor am I out of it.

Sometimes stay with friends in South London and travel in from Wandsworth Town Station. An infernal malebolge which makes our journey seem dangerously alluring. A pure ordeal, undisguised by any trappings of luxury. The comatose consciousness penetrated only by the savage slamming of a hundred doors. Uncompromising, unequivocal, absolute nadir of commuting.

Notebook's disjointed form fits it not only to be written by commuters, but also to be read by them, in small doses as required. Aim: to produce a subversive work which will infiltrate trains everywhere and prompt mass desertion. Slogan: Commuters of the world unite! You have nothing to lose but your trains!

'Special announcement' made in broad regional English at Oxford: 'If there are any German people on the station, will they please call at the Travel Centre for a message.' Doubtless there ensued a stampede of Germans all speaking fluent English. A similar summons for English people in Bavarian German at, say, München Hauptbahnhof would surely provoke no response whatsoever.

DIALOGUE 3
'Hello, what are you doing these days?'
'I'm still commuting.'
'You want to be careful. Too much of that sort of thing can make you blind.'

MORE TRAVELLING TITLES
The Roughshooter's Dog. Speed Records on Britain's Railways. The Enterprise as a Learning System. Electron Spin Resonance Spectrometers. Ulcer Department (printed on folder). The Organisation of the In-Patient's Day. Industrial Society: Class, Cleavage and Control.

Oxford to Paddington inclusive – a total of 27 stations. 3^3, a potentially mystic number, but no chance of commuters releasing any of the magic power.

OBIT 11

Conscious of death's approach, he took
His glasses off and closed his book
(Whodunnit he would never know),
Switched off the little radio,
Removed his wrist-watch and false teeth;
Relieved of these, drew his last breath.

Catch 0712 so frequently that 0815 the other day was like a holiday for me. M. brought me hot coffee from buffet. Sun, that much higher an hour later, streamed in. A. was putting finishing touches to a *nunchaku*, a karate weapon consisting of two pieces of wood joined by a cord. J. opened briefcase to reveal children's interlocking coloured plastic bricks for use on a course for businessmen – 'they have to build a profitable tower which must stand up long enough to be measured'. They consider themselves to be on an early train. I deem it degenerately late. Life on 0712 much more – all too – real and earnest. Good to be reminded of *autres trains, autres moeurs*.

ANTI-KONTAKION 8

A curse on the train. Aura reducer. Tension producer. Frightening crew of ghosts and ghouls. Enlightening clue to Aristotle's rules. Novel portraying shadowy roles. Devil delaying gathering souls. Anathema sit.

Priests, bishops even, sometimes commute. They treat the train as a means of transport. They do not see it for what it is – a field full of folk, working and travelling as the world expects, poised between the choice tower and the dreadful dungeon – a field full of all manner of men, ripe for their labours. These shepherds of souls dress and deport themselves like businessmen. They usually turn out to have administrative jobs in an office called Church House, which they ingenuously assume to be as well-known as the Houses of Parliament.

Tale told me on train of rise and fall of an officious Oxford ticket-collector. He would go to any lengths to prevent people travelling without tickets, even if they were known to him as regulars, and even though you can always buy a ticket on the train. Calling in the assistance of a large policeman was the least of his ploys. On one occasion he seized the briefcase of a victim, skipped across the tracks, and deposited it in the left-luggage office on the opposite platform. To redeem his property the owner, who could not legally cross the rails, had to negotiate the notorious Oxford tunnel, and thus missed his train.

One day this persecutor of passengers received his come-uppance. A beautiful girl in an expensive fur coat – who knows, her name may have been Zuleika – arrived from London ticketless. The man stopped her at the barrier and began to fulminate and threaten with all the fanatical fervour of a fundamentalist preaching hell-fire. The girl interrupted his tirade saying calmly: 'I have no ticket to give you. Will you accept *this* instead?' Whereupon she opened her coat to reveal total nakedness. At this sight the man cracked. He collapsed whimpering in his sentry-box, was removed, and has never been seen again.

'Will the Island Supervisor telephone the A.F.O.' 'Will the A.S.M. contact the A.M.O.' 'Will the B.V.M. telephone the I.H.S.' 'Will the I.C.B.M. intercept the U.F.O.' 'Will the P.M. report to the H.P. immediately.' 'Will the K.G.B. surrender to the S.I.S.' Q: Which of these announcements are not genuine? A: Try again. They are all genuine. Only the most hubristic commuter would deny having heard them all and many others like them. Very probably the Last Trump will first be heard over the tannoy at Paddington Station.

COMMUTER'S CALENDAR 2
2 April: Snow. Strike. Stoppages.

Notice near Old Oak Common, flat on wall beside railway where drivers can only see it if they happen to look sideways as they pass: KEEP ENGINES AS QUIET AS POSS-IBLE.

For excitement, truck-spotting beats engine-spotting any day. Marshalling-yards resemble lakes where the hamax-ologist, after several blank days, may suddenly glimpse a gaggle of transient Polybulks or a skein of migrating Proditti Agricoli among the flocks of common Hops and Vans. Peter Scott at Slimbridge runs a scheme whereby, for a small fee, you can have a wild fowl assigned to you and be kept informed of its movements. It is known as duck-adoption. British Rail could boost their revenue and give a lot of innocent pleasure by instituting truck-adoption. I have known an Experimental Clear Roof, originally ringed at Westbourne Park, turn up weeks later in sidings at Oxford, and have noted a Salmon from Ashford, Kent, in Hinksey yards. At Didcot, the hamaxological equivalent of Tring reservoir, I once saw a To Work Within South Wales And Monmouthshire Only.

HEADLINE 1
Western Region Trains Pruned.

Another P.N. analogue: John Fowles's *The Aristos*. A fine specimen of the genre which Fowles must have found harder and more satisfying to write than any of his novels. Judged by my own admittedly arbitrary criteria, it displays perhaps too much premeditation and not enough of the randomness of a notebook. Most writing attempts to impose an artificial order on the true order of creation (mistakenly called chaos by some). The Premeditated Notebook, as I define it, attempts to reflect this true order. The form lends itself to the avoidance of superimposed organisation. Fowles has flawed a brilliant book by selecting this form and then systematically obliterating one of its chief advantages. In his introduction he disingenuously writes: 'The book you are about to begin is written in the form of notes. This is not laziness on my part,' (accepted – writing a P.N. is hard work) 'but an attempt to suppress all rhetoric, all persua-sion through style.' No. I might have come closer to believing him if he had offered his thoughts as they occurred to him, instead of deliberately rearranging them in tenden-tious patterns of numbered paragraphs. Even then, as

Fowles happily demonstrates, you cannot escape style by writing notes. The style is the notebook is the man.

Depressing dead days between Christmas and New Year. Melancholy. The world's whole sap is sunk. I think of Lenin sealed in his train like a bacterium. Of Tolstoy, self-banished from his home, dying at the station-master's house at Astapovo. Of Nietzsche's postcard sent to a friend from Turin Station on 4 January 1889: 'Sing a new song for me: the world is transfigured and all the heavens rejoice. The Crucified.'

British stations never contribute to history or philosophy or legend. To stand on a railway platform in central Europe is to experience an exhilarating feeling of open options, of freedom to travel in any direction, of receptiveness to ideas from every culture. But to stand on a station in England, especially at this suspended midwinter moment, prompts nothing but inward-looking meditations on death and madness.

> Like truthless dreams, so are my joys expired,
> And past return are all my dandled days.
>
> (Ralegh)

Espinas, the anthropologist, quoted by Lévi-Strauss: 'The management of a great railroad company is not a social reality at all.' How much less, then, can a trainload of commuters claim recognition as a social reality or as any kind of existing entity?

TRACKSIDE INDUSTRY 4

Hamlet Furniture. Not too far from Stoke Poges, so perhaps they specialise in the kind of thing our rude forefathers sat on. Or do they make stuff less antique yeoman than Dane? Once noticed outside Hamlet's premises a pantechnicon with REST ASSURED in big letters on the side. Wonder if it contained a flight of singing angels?

OBIT 12

Within his melancholy hearse
They drove away the universe,

> *A candle in a pumpkin head,*
> *The world expired when he was dead.*

One thing worse than washing and tinkering with the car on Sunday – talking about it in the train on Monday.

Have had a total block for about three months. It began with Futter and Witter who, at the time of writing, lord it over Paddington and Oxford. Can never remember which is which. That does not matter. They are as interchangeable as Tweedledum and Tweedledee. A prominent mug-shot of the Paddington one used to obstruct us as we poured off the train – it was mounted on a kind of sandwich-board in the middle of the platform. It soon sprouted a beard and other embellishments. Eventually it disappeared. As for the Oxford one, as far as I know, I have never set eyes on him or his reproduced likeness.

Anyway, the block arose because I wanted to make a rhyme about the obviously factitious names Futter and Witter. Inspiration never came. Could get no further than:

> Said Mr Futter to Mr Witter,
> Let's meet at Reading for a pint of bitter;

or:

> 'Oh Mr Witter,' said Mr Futter,
> 'I've just invented a camera shutter.
> Please oblige me, Mr Witter,
> And be my experimental sitter.'

Thank God for the dynamite of prose. But my escape campaign has been retarded by three wasted months. Now another spring finds me still languishing. Spring, when etiolated commuters stand out like dead elms. Spring, wherein each thing renews, save only the commuter. Our sap fails to rise. Yet we yearn. How we yearn.

Donnish type insisted on catechising Indonesian student sitting opposite him struggling with Orwell's *Nineteen Eighty-Four*. Despite obvious incomprehension on pupil's part, the travelling academic waffled on: 'It's quite close now and much has already come true.'

Yes. Trainspeak. Trainthink. Trainwashing. The train: our ubiquitous Big Brother. The train vaporizes rebels, makes us unpersons. Obediently we mouth: 'Freedom is Slavery', 'We are the dead', until the day of realisation that we love the train.

Orwell foresaw it all: loudspeakers blaring a humourless mixture of musak and disinformation. Twenty-four-hour digital clocks. Trainspeak coinages like Inter-City, Travellers-Fare, Awayday, Railair, Sealink, Britainshrinkers, Motorail, Winterbreak, Railcard, Seaspeed, Golden Rail, Stardust Mini Holiday, High Speed Train, and Warnpass. Television screens displaying reports of the latest achievements of B.R. Portraits of officials. Propaganda about technological advances, service to the public, improved facilities.

Orwell even foresaw me furtively scribbling in this Notebook:

He had carried it guiltily home in his briefcase. Even with nothing written in it, it was a compromising possession.

Paralysing thought: can we possibly escape? Even those of us lucky, bold, quixotic, stupid or mad enough to quit the physical train for good may find that, like Kavafy's city, the train follows us, cannot be shaken off. Orwell again:

Do not imagine that you will save yourself . . . What happens to you here is for ever . . . We shall crush you down to the point from which there is no coming back . . . Never again will you be capable of ordinary human feeling. Everything will be dead inside you.

Winston had no chance. But we have. We have entered the age of doublethink. True. But we can still outwit the Thought Police. We are not yet living in a Police Train. We have a duty to resist, to assert our individuality, our humanity; to fan our divine spark into a flame. Winston began his diary too late. With this Notebook may I be just in time. Curious that Winston and Julia set out on their last journey into love-making countryside from Paddington.

> Dictation, dictation, dictation,
> The donkey went down to the station.

Why did we chant that at school? It clearly refers to commuting. Note the tedious repetition in the first line, and the hint of something unpleasant imposed or dictated against one's will. For 'donkey' read 'commuter', a stubborn drudge of low IQ motivated to work a treadmill for life by a carrot that he cannot and will never see. A double-edged Pythian couplet.

We even have our own weather. Ersatz, instant – like railway tea and coffee. Crazily speeded up *à la* Buster Keaton or Charlie Chaplin. Ordinary sane human beings sit in their static homes or stroll outdoors in meteorological conditions that last long enough for them to observe: 'It's wet / sunny / warm / cold etc.' and to ruminate thereon. We rush headlong through storms and sunshine, fog and clear patches in an unnatural, disorienting way. We can never say what the weather *is*. A variation on the torture theme – the cigar and ice-cube technique.

ANTI-KONTAKION 9

A curse on the train. Vicious circle holding men in. Sealed transport balking Lenin. Harming ordeal for those inside every day. Charming ideal for those who ride to go away. Anathema sit.

One 31 December a Paddington announcer wished us a happy new year over the tannoy. Was going to say he *forgot himself* to the extent of wishing us a happy new year. But perceived the trap in time. 'They' slip in these calculated lapses every now and then as part of the softening-up process. We must strengthen our defences, increase our vigilance. Careless thought costs lives. Our lives.

On the Oxford run, the real crack-up begins on average after the first five years. By that time, however, few have sufficient perception left to recognise in themselves the symptoms. Moreover, of those few, only a handful want to face the truth. The others prefer to lapse into voluntary narcosis.

Notebook proceeds like an unpredictable train. Subject to frequent stoppages and breakdowns, it lags so far behind schedule that it can only crawl a few yards on rare occasions when track is clear of regular traffic. It limps from signal to signal, buffeted by slipstreams of passing expresses. Between two sentences, between two words, may gape a twelvemonth's chasm. Between the lines . . .

Daily penance – twenty-seven stations of the cross.

Bumped into J. one day shortly after I had started commuting. I was rushing to board the train and bag (by putting my bag on it – is that the derivation?) a seat.

'You won't last long like that,' he said. 'No hurry, no worry. If you can't spend a journey standing, or miss a train with equanimity, don't commute.'

I took the wrong part of his advice. I have schooled myself always (well, nearly always) to remain calm, to retain my sang-froid, my phlegm, come what may – a model commuter. Of course, what I should have done was give up commuting at once. Blaise Cendrars: '*La lutte pour la vie c'est la lutte pour la non-adaptation.*' Subject for dissertation: mental anguish in chameleons.

LITERARY LANDMARK 4, PANGBOURNE

Kenneth Grahame spent his last years here. He wrote The Wind in the Willows *when he lived at Cookham Dene, setting the book mainly in that big loop of the river which the railway castrates. Whimsical, sexless moles, toads and water-rats hold little interest for the commuter, but Kenneth Grahame himself does.*

His sad life stands as a warning to all those who, having seen the light to the extent of saying 'I must give up this futile existence', yet postpone the decisive severance until tomorrow.

Grahame worked in the Bank of England, and became its Secretary when he was 39. With Pagan Papers *and* The Golden Age *already published, he enjoyed a considerable literary reputation. Later he became more famous with* Dream Days *and* The Wind in the Willows. *In all his writings he kept reverting to his wish to quit the mercenary life of the City for the genuine values of the Thames and the Berkshire Downs. Yet he could never bring himself to practise what he preached. As his biographer, Peter Green, comments: 'The City owned at least half his soul . . . he needed his cage.'*

In 1908, aged 49, Grahame did at last exchange the Bank for the river bank. 'Yet,' writes Peter Green, 'here again we sense impending tragedy. He had waited too long and compromised too often.'

Posterity may not sit in judgement on Kenneth Grahame. Here was one for whom escape ought to have been easy. At a comparatively early age he had the money and the reputation, lack of which lesser mortals use as their excuse for not letting go. Still he procrastinated. Which pusillanimous one of us can blame him?

An eye-witness described his funeral in 1932 in Pangbourne church:

. . . perhaps the most touching thing of all were the flowers sent by children from all over the country, with cards attached in a childish scrawl, saying how much they loved him.

Those cards came about thirty years too late.

> I see a truth which once I quite ignored –
>   Just why the chain
> Is known as the *communication* cord,
>   Which stops the train.

Old commuters never die. They just go off the rails.

The devil himself, who, the enemy of all humour in the face of disaster, as of all human delight, and often disguised as a social worker for the common good . . . wants nothing so much as that man shall believe himself unfriended by any higher power than he.

(Malcolm Lowry)

Very relevant because:

a) Commuting constitutes a disaster for all involved in it.

b) More than most, commuters have little sense of the numinous.

c) The whole business discourages humour. Weep, and the train weeps with you. Laugh, and you receive withering looks from all sides.

Just as religion has its hour in church on Sunday, so humour is confined to certain television shows. The devil does not want either to impinge on our secular, working lives. He finds the train an ideal instrument for his Mephistophelean purposes. Let us fight him with deadly levity. Lawrence Durrell: 'Life is too important not to be taken lightly.'

LOOSE COUPLING 1
LOOSE COUPLING or INTER-CITY INTERCOURSE
(calling at all stations from Paddington to Oxford,
via Maidenhead Junction)

> *A lisping blond on Paddington*
> *Showed girls his royal oak,*
> *One left the train at Westbourne Park,*
> *Would not act on his joke.*

Western Glory – Western Ichabod.

Anything ever written about Paddington mentions that the area between the hotel and the buffers is known as 'the Lawn'. Hard to imagine a more sick parody of greensward. You cannot even sit down there any more. Announcers sometimes page a person known as 'the Lawn supervisor' who, I imagine, oversees the provision of linen and drapery with particular responsibility for the First Class antimacassars. But generally the arid asphalt is referred to as 'the station concourse'. This raises further semantic problems as my dictionary does not admit of 'concourse' meaning anything other than 'a crowd' or 'a confluence of things'. Maybe I should follow Notebook with a sequel to Chomsky entitled *Locomotive Grammar*, or to Gowers – *The Complete Train Words*.

All the sights we shall never see, because cuttings or buildings or vegetation block our view. All the people we see, sit with, even address, but shall never know, because convention or inhibition or prejudice restrain us. O why do we rush through the fields in trains, missing so much and so much?

Spring advances. Among less formal travellers open necks are winning the battle against scarves. By such humdrum signs we mark the passing seasons. *Pereunt et imputantur.*

DIALOGUE 4

R. (5th year commuter): 'Where are we?'
Self: 'Just outside Reading. Surely you know the route by now.'
R: 'Good God, man, I never look out of the window!'

As the years go by, find I read less and less. As I avert my gaze from woods, which recall my youth, so I recoil from books, which remind me of a time when I made free with ideas, rejoiced in the exercise of my mind, and aspired to lead a literary life. Now bad books irritate me. Good ones sadden me. It might have been.

Weary J., waking up reluctantly one morning on 0712 approaching Paddington: 'I sometimes wish this train would never stop.' To what an abject state the train reduces beings that were human once! Loath to set foot on the platform of life, we cling to the illusory comfort of our destroyer, seeking to prolong the insidious coma. 'Don't you wish we could go on for ever, and never stop?' No fringed surrey our conveyance. Our journey no Freudian last ride together. 'What if heaven be that we fixèd so, ever should so abide?' Not heaven in our case, but a hell so subtle that its very victims – voluntary Mazeppas – desire its continuance.

A bad day. Feel as though my door pins need greasing.

HEADLINE 2

Seasons Sent Reeling.

Unexplained delay at Didcot. (Nothing abnormal about that.) At last two uniformed soldiers board train. Handcuffed to one of them a pugnacious-looking, close-cropped, bedenimed youth. Train moves off. Law-abiding commuters look variously annoyed, smug, curious, compassionate, indifferent. We should not. And therefore never send to know. Casual travellers do not notice our handcuffs. Few of us sense the bracelets round our own wrists. But they are there, along with the uniformed escort. There, too, rigid rails and sharp ballast: iron bars and stone walls which do make a prison and a cage. Man is born free and is everywhere in trains.

At Didcot they make a thing of restoring steam engines. At Reading enthusiasts are renovating two scrapped diesel locomotives. At Old Oak Common, no doubt, fanatics are already busy revamping an obsolete Advanced Passenger Train. The nearer we come to London, the more time, like frenzied footage from an old film, accelerates.

To travel hopefully is a better thing than to arrive. Yes, but to arrive, hopefully, is a better thing than to travel. Even so do language and life develop.

No escape from routine even in small matters where we imagine ourselves free agents. It has slowly dawned on me over the years how frequently, having solved the crossword and read the news, I put down the paper, look out of the window, and see a certain row of young oaks along the edge of a green paddock with, beyond, a small cemetery containing a prominent crucifix with its back to the railway.

ANTI-KONTAKION 10
A curse on the train. Betrayer. Traitor. Treachery. Trickery. Stratagem. Artifice. Trap. Snare. Lure. Enticement. Bait. Decoy. Anathema sit.

Bountiful British Rail provides sugar lumps for the local horses and miniature bottles for the children to play at shops with. But at what a cost.

Better not to inquire why some trucks have chalked on the side the word: SCALPS.

LOOSE COUPLING 2
He pleaded quite appealingly,
More clumsily than well,

Calculate that I have certainly made my thousandth and two thousandth journeys, possibly even my three thousandth as well. Needless to say, not one of these milestones or millstones or tombstones has been marked in any way. No ticker-tape. No bunting. No champagne. No starlets. No fanfare from Futter. No welcome from Witter. No free season ticket. Non-events during the living death of a non-person.

Rock Island Line, Chattanooga Choo Choo, Last Train to San Fernando, 3.10 to Yuma, Canadian Pacific, Freight Train, The Runaway Train – countless songs about the railroads of the American continent. Europe has songs about trains too, usually wistful, poignant, romantic. But railways in Britain have produced no sub-culture (apart from the forgotten ballads of the navvies who built them). They are mundane, prosaic, sterile. Imagine a folk-singer belting out a piece on the 0712 to Paddington, or trying to convince his audience that British Rail (WR) is a mighty fine line. . .

Rudyard Kipling, in *The King*, tried to claim some romance for our railways:

> 'Romance!' the season-tickets mourn,
>   '*He* never ran to catch His train,
> 'But passed with coach and guard and horn –
>   'And left the local – late again!
> 'Confound Romance!' . . . And all unseen
>   Romance brought up the nine-fifteen.

Took me literally years to work out that He, with a capital aitch, was Romance, and that Romance was the King of the title. Even then this stanza remains obscure. Since the 'season-tickets' (interesting synecdoche) appear to believe that Romance went out with stagecoaches, the line 'And left the local – late again!' cannot refer to a local train, but must mean that Romance left the pub after drinking-up time on more than one occasion. However, Kipling goes straight to the point in the last two lines. 'All unseen' by the 'season-tickets', Romance may well have brought up the nine-fifteen in 1880, and may still bring it up in 1980 for all we know. We shall never find out because we can never wait for the nine-fifteen. Romance never has and never will bring up any trainload of commuters. Railway romance remains transatlantic or *outre-manche*. In Britain romance begins only when commuting stops.

Rabbits, birds, sheep, cattle, horses, scarcely stir as we pass. They fear not men in the woods because they see so few. They fear not trains in the fields because they see so many.

The train resembles a school or college with nervous new boys and arrogant old hands. Different years tend to stick together. But, unlike students, we have no goal, no prospects. Even a borstal offers more incentives. A prisoner-of-war camp furnishes a closer parallel. *Stalag Zug 0712*. We swap accounts of our capture, question newcomers on the progress of the war, reminisce about our days of freedom. Most of us fear the authorities too much to attempt a break-out. Although we have committed no crime, we feel an irrational sense of guilt as we cower in our compartments, hoping that the jackboots will not stop at our door.

HEADLINE 3

Windham Railroads To Victory.
(Chambers gives the verb as a U.S. usage meaning 'to push forward fast'. 'To get nowhere slowly' might be nearer the mark.)

Remember once returning from a holiday in Greece – a brown, unshaven, dirty undergraduate with a head full of exotic memories. Caught the 1715 or its equivalent at Paddington, and treated myself to tea in the restaurant. What impressed me most was not the toasted tea-cake, but the obvious commuters (who could still afford to take the full tea every day). Demigods they seemed, wearing well-cut suits, endowed with fine crania crammed with weighty matters. Some twenty years have elapsed since then. Have commuters changed? Or has commuting simply removed the scales of innocence from my eyes? Today I see myself and my companions as utterly ungodlike – butterflies broken on flanged wheels.

Evil communications corrupt. Good communications corrupt absolutely.

Might as well abandon attempts to dream up fantasies. A few days after jotting idea of fanatics restoring obsolete Advanced Passenger Train, found this in *Times*:

Research and development for the train, costing so far about £10M, has (*sic*) been carried out mainly by a four-car experimental version which last year set a new British rail speed record of 152 mph. British Rail said yesterday that in 22,000 miles it had proved the advanced passenger train design principles satisfactorily and would now be pensioned off to the Railway Museum at York.

It is men who make a city, not walls or ships without crews (Nicias, with an echo of Alcaeus). Not true of the trenocosm. World that is not world. The train's metal walls mould us into automata. Commuters could never 'make' the train. The train moves passengers, parcels, produce, without distinction. The train asserts and imposes itself, absorbs us. Men bring dead cities or ships to life, give them *raison d'être*. The train deprives men of reason and being. A hollow mockery of the ancient Greek ideal. A Trojan iron horse with death in its belly – death for us who fondly attempt to use it as a stratagem for invading the metropolis.

'The train approaching Platform 1 will be the 0712 to Paddington.' Will it? What is it now? What if it leaves late? At what point does it a) become, b) cease to be, the 0712? Will it still be the 0712 when it arrives at Paddington in an hour or so's time? What is the 0712? Does it have a continuous existence, or is it a mere ephemeron, dying and being born anew every day? Does it exist at all? Can we prove that it does? Can A.J. Ayer prove that it does not?

Reading, in the train, Malcolm Lowry, lover of digressions between commas in long sentences, and loadstone for involved coincidences. Lowry has piece on writer of a novel about animals destined for zoo on board ship. This writer, incidentally, we learn, once wrote 'about the factory chimneys of Eleusis' – as did I. I also had published in *Blackwood's Magazine* an account, entitled 'Recollections of a Train-Band Captain', of travelling through Yugoslavia in a luggage-van with a drugged lion and two eagle owls in cages on their way to Split Zoo. Minor coincidence: the parallels between Lowry's subject-matter and mine. Major coincidence: that, some twenty years ago, my first sustained article to be published should have been about a railway journey and the theme of freedom and captivity. Then, carefree, I pitied the lion. Today, the caged, doped creature, with intimations of dignity fast fading, is I.

How often does someone point to an unoccupied seat and inquire: 'Is anyone sitting there?' Usually the question receives a civil answer, yet it could only really be justified coming from Macbeth in the presence of Banquo's ghost.

Useful hint for impatient heirs: A Senior Citizen Railcard Gift Token Makes The Going Easy.

Commuting like ours leaves little time or energy for social life off the train. We run risk of forgetting existence of forms of human intercourse other than our own debased mode. For us 'non-commuter' comes to equal 'outsider'. Yet we are the true outsiders, outcasts. Notebook – among other things – a reply to Colin Wilson's *The Outsider*. Commuters stand the concept on its head. Compared with us, the outsider, the desperado, *l'étranger, o xenos*, have no problems. We look so ordinary, so respectable, and suffer so much – often without realising it ourselves, being deprived of all yardsticks or touchstones. We need contact with real people. We need frequent subjection to the therapeutic amazement of normal humans when they learn that we travel to work from Oxford to London and back every day. But *per se* the commuting denies us opportunities to see our lunatic selves as others see us. Blinkered, we travel on.

LOOSE COUPLING 3

As he went west, the girl went south
All flustered in a haze,
While hurling tons of oaths at him
Which left him in a daze.

A traxiom: every train has two sides. Like chickens in our unquestioning acceptance of the need to get from A to B, our proclivity to prefer barleycorns to gems, our capability of continued locomotion after death, and our general stupidity, we do not share with them the useful accomplishment of seeing out of both sides of the head at once. We can only cope with the view from one side of the train at a time. We alternate sides, though not regularly – only through irregularity can we hope to steal a march on the well-ordered, unimaginative enemy. It takes years, years, to collate and match the two sides, to be able to say immediately, at any point, what lies opposite the scene we are looking at. (The painstaking work of the long-term prisoner who knows he has all too many empty hours to while away.) An occasional ride at the front of a Diesel Multiple Unit, gazing past the driver straight down the tracks, vouchsafes new connections. A broken zip-fastener, we flash along, linking the disparate for a moment, leaving division in our wake.

On Oxford platform: live chicks chirping inside cartons marked *oeufs*. Which came first? Hatched after dispatch?

Dreamed I had published book entitled *Murder in the Cathedrals Express*.

Commuter palimpsests: the implacable stylus of the train, crossing and recrossing the parchment, renders the original manuscript illegible, irretrievable.

ANTI-KONTAKION 11

A curse on the train. Land without soil where seasons reel. Desert where toil new peasants conditioned not to feel. Pressurised system. Sterilised wisdom. Anathema sit.

On a red mini-tractor at Didcot and on certain wagons: For Use On Brute Circuit Only. Revelation dawned one morning at Oxford where a chalked notice: Danger, Keep Away, Do Not Move These Brutes, was propped, not against a crate of Dobermann pinschers, but beside three or four trolleys which were supporting a broken fence. So Brute, disappointingly, equals something like British Rail Utility Trolley. Nevertheless, I still think I'll give the Brute Circuit a miss this year. *Et tu?*

Department of statistics: railway crosses Thames six times, at Maidenhead, Goring, Moulsford, Appleford, Culham, and Oxford. It also crosses two or three sections of the Grand Union Canal; the River Brent at Hanwell; the River Colne at West Drayton; two branches of the River Loddon at Twyford; and Foudry Brook at Reading. NB: the number of place-names containing the element 'ford'. NB: for good measure, the much greater number of names not containing 'ford'.

OXFORD STATION 1
OXFORD STATION
(A Fifth Quartet)

'Our little systems have their day.'
A.L. Tennyson

(A few hundred yards outside Oxford Station used to stand a billboard bearing the legend: 'The Nuffield Organisation Welcomes You To Oxford'.)

(Chemin de fer: *A game of chance*)

I

In the mid hour of the night,
Cupping my hand over my forehead
And breathing on the frosted pane,
Alone amid upholstery
(For Stetson, mon semblable, *alighted at Didcot),*
I peer, past a singing lamp-standard,

79

> *Past a coal-bunker and a pile of clinkers,*
> *To where, beneath the visiting moon,*
> *This world is crumbled out againe to his Atomies*
> *In graves of the Oxford cemetery.*
> *I have been here before.*
> *Or, in the interests of accuracy,*
> *Perhaps I should say someone has been here before.*
> *In time past I was here,*
> *In time future I shall be here,*
> *When I reach the station*
> *I shall be everywhere and nowhere.*
> *But here, now, night strikes on England,*
> *Night on Oxford town,*
> *And I, I am some otherwhere.*

How shall I know when Notebook is finished? What sign may I expect? At the moment can see no end, as fair copy lags further and further behind rough jottings. Perhaps I shall penelopize indefinitely in an attempt to cheat postnatal depression.

'Charlbury, Kingham, Moreton-in-Marsh and Worcester Shrub Hill standing at Platform Two.' Yes, and Birnam Wood standing at Dunsinane.

Commuter divers: daily groping for treasure in muddy waters and surfacing with old boots. The train a decompression chamber operated by a sadist who always brings us up too fast, cackling as he sees us smitten by caisson disease.

MYSTERY 9
Train creeping along through cloudburst. Suddenly, in middle of nowhere, standing on tracks, a drenched, donkey-jacketed man slowly waving up and down a yellow flag as big as a tablecloth. Could he be Enderby of PWM gang 42?

Saw John Wain one evening as I returned from work. 'Ah, back from the London nod, eh?' he muttered knowingly. Later he said he had no knowledge of such an expression, and denied having used it. A poetic description of commuting, all the same.

News that a man charged with murder, due to be tried at Oxford, will be accommodated at Oxford Prison because it would be 'unfair' to expect him to travel from Leicester or Winchester every day of a five-day week. Reasonable enough. But is it any less unfair to expect us, equally on trial, with our lives at stake, to cover 120 miles a day? On trial, did I say? Condemned, rather. No justice.

Next Sunday's colour supplements can be seen on the move as early as Tuesday. Conversely, commuters may be found doggedly doing last Sunday's papers as late as Friday.

Building by Paddington that cuts sky as sharply and cleanly as those great blades one used to find in hayricks.

Only by treating it as a cocoon can we derive any benefit from the train. We enter it as larvae, as gentle men. Most never progress beyond this stage, the stage of the grub, the dull drudge. ('Grub', says the dictionary, is probably cognate with 'grave'.) By mental effort we have to turn ourselves into chrysalids (dictionary: form taken by insect in the torpid stage of passive development between larva and imago; Greek, literally 'golden thing') before our minds atrophy – then bide our time.

That versatile polymath, Dr Theodore Stephanides, takes up the story:

Inside the horny envelope of the pupa, the whole caterpillar melts and deliquesces into an amorphous semi-liquid pulp until nothing of the original form remains. Viewed as a sentient entity, that caterpillar has 'died'. It has no organs with which to contact the outside world, no nervous system to afford it an awareness, however dim, of its own existence.

Yet, miraculously, the imago (the vocabulary shares the magic of the process) emerges as a butterfly, for which, as Dr Stephanides reminds us, the Greek is *psyche* or 'soul'. A true commutation. The only possible justification for entering the cocoon train in the first place.

LOOSE COUPLING 4

Alone in his compartment, he
Was straightening his dress,
When 'Will you sleep with me?' inquired
A winsome Scottish lass.

Unconsciously we are all the time having our senses of value and priorities warped. If, for example, 'They' remove a coach we have grown accustomed to, we become upset out of all proportion. Occasional travellers sit among us impervious to the undercurrents. For them, the train is a means of getting somewhere. For us, it *is* somewhere – and nowhere.

What have these in common: Castle, Tournament, Knights and Heralds, Beeches, Riverside, Flightpath, Triangle, Isis, Spires?

K., a chartered surveyor, goes into raptures over large warehouse at Reading. To me the place used to look like an outsize brick and concrete barn. K.'s professional appreciation makes me see it in new light. My turn now to try to open in other directions the eyes of K. and his kind.

MYSTERY 10

One quiet Monday evening on 1815, non-stop (significant, this) Paddington to Oxford, M. moved up to front of train to edit tapes. She noticed nothing untoward, yet on her way back down the train, half an hour or so later, she came upon an empty, comprehensively vandalised compartment – windows broken, fittings smashed, seats ripped. In the absence of any stereotyped hooligans, we concluded that a sober-suited fellow-commuter must have gone berserk, or even done the thing in cold blood, before quietly moving, frustration relieved, to another compartment.

Limits of a diesel's repertoire: playing On Ilkley Moor Baht'at, and blowing the occasional fume ring.

Disused tracks beckon like tempting backwaters. Good spots for courting engine-drivers or picnicking guards. Up the lazy branch-line on a Sunday afternoon.

Heath Robinson machinery for ballast-cleaning, long chord levelling and lining, and general track maintenance. Elegant, exceedingly intricate, and foreign. British Rail allows this apparatus to retain its exotic yellow livery, which brightens the dullest siding. The Mainliner Universal fascinates me. In U.S. slang, mainlining means injecting a narcotic into a principal vein. Mainliner = drug addict. Not sure how that ties up with the machine, but it certainly connects with commuting.

Travelling daily on the railways induces narcosis, turns us into mainliners, whence the term. Ironic that the dropout hooked on drugs finds himself reproducing the worst features of the life from which he sought escape. Little to choose in the end between commuting and pumping heroin into your system. Better, perhaps, the pure despair and pariah status of addiction than the spurious respectability of the train.

Incidentally, the Mainliner Universal has a notice on the side which warns: Ensure Sirens Working Before Operating Machine. What hazards lie in wait for us! We should never have left Ithaca in the first place.

In the buffet-car on the 1715 one evening, A. saw a pretty girl with exceptional legs. She alighted at Didcot. As he sat waiting for the train to start again, he observed the girl entering the Dragon Hotel opposite the station. Pausing only to make a bet with the sceptical steward, A. got off the train and made for the hotel. He bought the girl a drink, arranged to meet her again, left when her parents arrived to collect her, and caught a later train to Oxford.

Not for A. the wistful mopings of Palinurus:

She was bare-legged, and wore sandals, a green corduroy suit and a linen coat. With an intolerable sense of frustration I watched her out of sight: *'o toi que j'eusse aimée'*.

He hurried undithering down the Didcot stairs. No *esprit de l'escalier* for him. 'I'd like to make a permanent record of those pins,' he said, 'I really would.'

ANTI-KONTAKION 12

A curse on the train. Place beyond the thought-barrier where ideas are turned upside-down. World beyond the word-barrier where language operates inside-out. Cockpit beyond the sound-barrier where instruments work back-to-front. Anathema sit.

Diesel locomotives festooned in front with swaying pizzles. Trucks too. When uncoupled they twitch suggestively.

People who talk most loudly invariably the most boring. Those with interesting things to say do not wish to share them with the class. They speak softly, sparingly. Often they do not speak at all, but sit with strange eyes, keeping their visions bottled up inside them, impervious to those loudly proclaiming: 'I know a short cut – well, actually it's two miles longer, but if you keep your foot down and know the road etc. etc. etc.'

'Owing to an earlier incident at Southall, all trains into and out of Paddington will be subject to delays.' What lay behind this constantly intoned formula? The television screen, labelled Rail News, that evening inscrutably displayed the scorecard of England v. West Indies at Lord's. Had Greenidge hit a colossal six from St John's Wood to Southall? In the end an engine-driver told me he believed someone had 'gone under a train'. England: 250, West Indies: 182. An earlier incident.

> But at my back I always hear
> Time's Western Chariot hurrying near.

MYSTERY 11

Paddington announcement calling for 'the Russian car hire'. Recognisable by the snow on their tyres?

> I have seen the Mermaids shunting, each to each.
> I do not think that they will sing . . .

At Paddington, trains go out like the sea, leaving pools of oil, disinfectant, and incontinent urine. Beachcombing rats scuttle along the tideline.

Snatches of verse among the pieces of prose; green leaves in a bunch of cowslips.

Curious experience, for me, of writing Notebook by hand. Normally I type everything. I find inditing in longhand painful, slow, tiring, unfavourable to the flow of ideas. Yet its being all those things and more makes it the ideal method for Notebook. When typing, I feel like a boffin who manipulates mechanical claws behind a glass partition. The lack of physical contact with pen, ink, paper, engenders unreality and encourages glibness, digressions, verbosity, megalomania. (See my thesis on influence of typewriter on modern literature.) Whereas, when I write manually, my reluctance to make any more effort than absolutely necessary forces upon me a lapidary conciseness. Pain hones thought. Typewriter kicks up such a racket too. Using a pen, I can hear myself think, feel myself write – each word tangible. I spurn the rotivator, favour the spade.

LOOSE COUPLING 5
'For I've a yen for a lang, lang lay,
Look, mon, my bra I slough,
As for my panties, bide a wee
And I will burn 'em now!

People use term 'shuttle service', but have they ever seen a loom? Endlessly the train clatters to and fro, to and fro, to and fro, weaving the fabric of commuters' coarse, grey lives.

LITERARY LANDMARK 5, READING GAOL
This ominous building stands symbolically at the mid-point of our path. Ironically, its architecture differs little from that of the adjacent biscuit factory – except that the biscuit factory is arguably the more prison-like of the two. It resembles a child's toy fort with its quaint brick towers and crenellation. Its harmless appearance renders it the more sinister when we know that from it issued Oscar Wilde's

Ballad *and his* De Profundis. *We have only to glimpse it to be reminded that each man kills the thing he loves, and that commuting is a pretty comprehensive method of doing this, of destroying self, family, and freedom. Today public opinion might not censure Oscar Wilde, and the law might not imprison him. But he himself would be quick to satirise our smug concepts of progress and enlightenment. No doubt he would turn a few epigrams on the ingenious forms of imprisonment we continue to devise for ourselves.*

Remarkable morning: Announcement at Oxford that 0815 was running 45 minutes late 'due to a token failure at Evesham'. We soon ascertained that the expression did not signify a symbolic breakdown. But the truth remained bizarre.

Engine-drivers may not proceed along a stretch of single track without first procuring a token which proves the line clear. In this case, we learned, the system had broken down because someone had taken the token home by mistake. In the not-so-old days, this procedure took the form of a charming, clumsy courtship display, involving the handing over of a large metal and leather true lovers' knot. Today, more prosaically, drivers obtain the prophylactic token from an automatic dispenser.

As we mulled over all this information, gathered from various members of the station staff, we heard another announcement telling us not to worry about the delay because 'a service will be held at Didcot'. A token requiem for the 0815?

Notice near Reading Station: All Descending Goods And Mineral Trains Must STOP DEAD Here.

After many journeys, we become sensitive to subtle differences brought about by a change of track. A shift to left or right means that we can – or cannot where we did before – look down an embankment, read a notice, see past a building, over a tree, and so on. We turn to our neighbours and remark: 'So we're on the slow line today then', feeling slightly reassured that we are not yet so far gone that such fine details escape us, yet at the same time depressed that we have reached the stage of observing and commenting upon such trivia. He was a man who used *not* to notice such things.

TRAIN GAME 5

We can count flowers as well as birds. Rose-bay willowherb, ragwort, cow parsley and the umbellifers, buttercup, yarrow, wormwood (wormwood!), mullein, moon daisy, primrose, bluebell, meadowsweet, cowslip, wild rose, bedstraw, toadflax, scabious, knapweed, thistle, evening primrose. Speed blurs the flowers, blurs the seasons: green, gold, brown, black, flow past (everything flows), merge into a composite streak, the synthetic season of our tickets.

As one recognises a friend at a distance by gait or stance, by indefinable aura, so we identify flowers, whose petals we have no time to number, by their quiddity, learned in the spaciousness of youth, stored, and now retrieved in this cramped futility of what ought to be our fruitful years. Botanising on our own graves.

Chelsea Flower Show; Oxford University terms and vacations; Smithfield Show; the Motor Show; holidays and terms of Radley, the Dragon, Cheltenham Ladies', Malvern; General Synod; the annual conference of the Women's Institute; Test matches; – all these events and more impinge upon our awareness with influxes of unbelievably true-to-type characters.

Posh-speaking, g-droppin' county ladies discussing gardens and comparing gardeners; undergraduates and students – two different breeds; Herefordshire farmers with broad accents and slow speech; motor car buffs in sharp suits, loudly boasting of the performance of their vehicles in amoebean contest; blasé or bohemian Kensington and Hampstead parents bidding gushing farewell to their priggish brats, who share our thankfulness that Mummy and Daddy do not accompany them on the train; well-intentioned, retired, upper-middle-class Christians, the only lay-people fitted to deal with the procedural *longueurs* of ecclesiastical policy-making; completely typical W.I. committee-women impassively ticking off items on the agenda: abortion, dress-making, pre-marital sex, flower-arrangement; chivalrous, middle-aged gentlemen in MCC ties who

seek permission from any women in the compartment
before lighting their pipes or removing their jackets.

We patronise them, snigger at them in self-defence.
Anything to silence the insistent inner voices telling us that
we cut much more laughable, pitiable figures than these
seasonal travellers. Telling us that we appear to these
worthy people as hollow, two-dimensional, stereotyped
commuters. Telling us the truth.

ANTI-KONTAKION 13

*A curse on the train. Dungeon with engine. Push-me-pull-you.
Crush-me-kill-you. Hollow Halloween pumpkin. Troop-laden*
Potemkin. *Suicide ride. Doom of the dead. Home of the mad.*
Anathema sit.

MYSTERY 12

*A covered wagon sits permanently in a bay at Didcot Station. On its
side the words: Passenger, For Internal Use Only, Area Manager,
Didcot.*

The black rabbit in the goose field always used to squat
beside a thick, bosky hedge. Now they have razed the
hedge, burnt the remains, ploughed in the evidence, and
put up a barbed-wire fence. You can almost see the border-
guards on their high wooden platforms, searchlights and
machine-guns at the ready. Meanwhile, in its formerly
sheltered position, now totally exposed, the black rabbit
still crouches.

LOOSE COUPLING 6

'Tap low my maidenhead,' she begged.
'I'll twy for devilwy,'
Our hero lisped, and very soon
Was treading manfully.

HEADLINE 4

Death Benefit Scene Still Changing.

Significance of simple truths slowly sinks in. When we
board train, we can sit on either side. We can also sit facing,

or with our backs to, our destination. Thus we can see the whole sixty-mile landscape advancing or retreating – see everything increasing in size and speed as it rushes towards us, or growing smaller and slower as it recedes. The fact that we make the journey in two directions each day opens further options: we can travel east, facing east or west; we can travel west, facing west or east. We have a choice of eight basic seating positions, whether the train has compartments or open coaches. Over the years we discover the alternatives. There seem so many possibilities. But the major revelation comes – if it comes at all – when we realise that, while in the world endless possibilities exist, in the train they are strictly limited. Once we perceive these limits, these restrictions, we are half-way towards winning back our freedom.

Before we plunge into the tunnel of winter darkness, and for a period after we emerge, we journey through a leafless landscape. Foliage and vegetation encroach or diminish so slowly that we scarcely notice the subtle alterations in our daily outlook. By midsummer we have quite forgotten what lies beyond the trees, forgotten that we ever knew.

Commuterus Vulgaris Ferrovianus, Prasinus: the only species in the world that both hibernates and aestivates.

Maytime effusion, outside alliterative calendar: cow parsley, chestnut candles, dog daisies, hawthorn frostwork; vivid patches of yellow mustard – smell filling carriage. Unapproachable, heart-rending beauty.

Paddington announcers lie in their teeth about certain trains. They say: 'Didcot will be the first stop' of some trains which always call at Reading. They could easily use an ambiguous formula, but they plump for the lie direct. Does it sit heavily on their consciences? At all events, undeterred Reading regulars happily crowd aboard.

Repetition can be good or bad. Through endlessly repeating the name of Jesus, Orthodox monks attain a high mystic state – cf. the Buddhist chant of *om mane padme hum*. Repetitiveness of commuting parodies such methods. It leads not to *satori* or *nirvana*, but to doltish insensibility and absurd pseudo-revelations, such as that DORMAR = RAMROD backwards, or that every train has two sides and two directions.

In Buddhist terms, the train rather symbolises the Wheel of Things 'whose compartments are all the heavens and hells, and all the chances of human life' (*Kim*). All commuters need release from the fire-carriage, but few of us realise this, few even begin to 'tread the way of deliverance'. We require enlightened lamas, first to show us how we are bound – 'See here the Hell appointed for avarice and greed. Flanked upon the one side by Desire and on the other by Weariness' – and then to expound the possibilities of salvation.

The lama in *Kim* knew that, to obtain his release from the Wheel, he had to find the River of the Arrow. At one point he said: 'But that the *rêl*-carriage fills my head with noises of devil-drums I would go in it to Benares now . . . Yet by so going we may miss the River.' Precisely. By so going we miss the river every day. As I have noted, it repeatedly offers itself to us, and we constantly reject its approaches.

The brown god is almost forgotten
By the dwellers in cities – ever, however, implacable,
Keeping his seasons and rages, destroyer, reminder
Of what men choose to forget. Unhonoured, unpropitiated
By worshippers of the machine, but waiting, watching and
    waiting.

(T.S. Eliot)

I hereby utter a Beowulfian *beot* – that if I am liberated or liberate myself from the bondage of the Flanged Wheel, I will make a pilgrimage on foot along the course of my captivity, paying especial homage to the reproachful Thames – an act of penance and thanksgiving.

Has anyone written a thesis on train-symbolism in Rudyard Kipling's *Kim*? If not, I offer the subject *gratis*:

'This is the work of devils!' said the lama ... He stood in a gigantic stone hall paved, it seemed, with the sheeted dead – third-class passengers who had taken their tickets overnight.

'Enter! This thing is the work of the Government.'

'There is not one rule of right living which these *te-rains* do not cause us to break.'

'A wonderful matter is the *te-rain*.'

Discuss.

If these notes read like the work of a tired man; if they appear to sag under

> The heavy weight of many a weary day
> Not mine, and such as were not made for me;
> (Wordsworth)

then I have succeeded in conveying something of the essence of commuting.

When the train passes any kind of sporting activity – during my stretch I have seen cricket, soccer, rugger, golf, tennis, archery, volley-ball, speedway, greyhound racing, aunt sally – invariably nothing is happening. The bowler is always about to bowl, the referee about to restart play, the archer poised to shoot. Nothing takes place before our profane gaze. At our uncouth advent, the initiates freeze into a *tableau vivant*, waiting for us to pass before they resume celebration of the mysteries. This inexplicable phenomenon underlines the lack of rapport between our unnatural train-existence and normal life outside. The Grecian Urn Syndrome.

Review, in *The Times*, by Philip Howard, of a new novel. Howard describes the hero as 'oppressed by commuter values', and comments: 'But, fiction apart, the real heroes of life are not those who drop out, but those who soldier on and civilize their ruts.'

No, no, no, absolutely no. First, commuters have no values. Just as gravity does not exist in spaceships, so values do not exist on the train. Our minds float in the vacuum. Weightlessness = witlessness. Orthodoxy is unconsciousness. Second, you cannot have a civilised rut, unless it be what the dictionary calls 'periodic sexual excitement of male deer, goat, ram, etc.'. A rut *per se* is not susceptible of civilisation; nor can you drop out of a rut, for if you find yourself in one then you have dropped out of life and need to climb back in. The archetypal rut of the train contains no heroes, only well-drilled automata, carriage-fodder, who, not reasoning why people like Philip Howard think we should, soldier on mindlessly into the Valley of Death.

Dear Notebook, you go to and fro in my Woolworth's plastic briefcase, both vademecum and viaticum.

We occasionally gossip with guards or talk to ticket-collectors, but we never engage engine-drivers in dialogue. Indeed, we seldom see them, seldom spare them a thought or a glance. If we make the journey in exceptionally fast time, D. may remark: 'Wacky Jack's on the job today', and this has become a sort of catchphrase among us. At least it acknowledges the existence of a human in the cab, albeit a kind of idealised Casey Jones figure.

I once spoke with an engine-driver during a strike – work kills conversation – and he was amazed to learn that people commuted daily between Oxford and London. Why, after all, should he know the constitution of his pay-load? Far better that he and his mate should remain splendidly incommunicado. Heaven preserve us from the sort of non-communications inflicted on their passengers by airline pilots.

At holiday times 'They' let us trusties out on parole. The system works beautifully from 'Their' point of view. 'They' give us just long enough to forget the horrors of the train, but not so long that we begin to think of never returning. (cf. Sam Weller's story of Number Twenty who, although given countless chances, could not bring himself to leave the Fleet Prison.) 'They' know too that 'They' have conditioned us to believe that heavy penalties await those who break parole. 'They' let our bodies stray, confident that 'They' hold our minds in thrall. I aim once and for all to call 'Their' bluff.

LOOSE COUPLING 7

'How tactile her strong fingers are!
How sweet her pang-born cries!'
He mused, while goring with a will
On her train-shaken thighs.

We even have a Salvation Army commuter, a middle-aged man who always wears his drab uniform and never smiles or speaks. One day I caught him behaving in true para-military manner, using elbows and briefcase to fight his way aboard the train before non-combatants occupied all the seats.

I take care to conceal from my fellow-commuters that a chield's amang them takin notes, although they have nothing to fear from me, nor I from them. The real enemy, the train, like the wind, cannot read. On reflection, I ascribe this secretiveness to apprehension lest someone should tell me I am writing twaddle. I do not want to know. As long as I can believe that I may be producing something worthwhile, so long can I lean on Notebook as a secret support. So long and no longer. Once someone rightly or wrongly calls my belief into question, this support will collapse and I with it.

As a boy I used to enjoy seeing from trains large advertisements plonked incongruously down in open country. I viewed as equally exciting white horses cut out of hillsides and white men cut out of hardboard, striding across fields, shouldering a ladder bearing the legend: Hall's Distemper. I responded to the surreal element in both.

Our route offers only one example of such alfresco publicity, and a pretty mundane one at that. In a meadow near Tilehurst stands a hoarding which, for a long time, used to proclaim enticingly: Your Name Could Be Here. Today it reads, most improbably: Corby New Town,

Northants, First In The Field For Industry And Housing.

It strikes me as odd that anyone should pay to display such a sign anywhere, but why they should choose to direct it at passengers on a stretch of line between Didcot and Reading passes all comprehension. If only we could have a few painters with ladders to brighten up our journey, but I fear that they have been misguidedly proscribed by those who consider billboards and trees mutually exclusive.

Thank goodness for the phasing out of claustrophobic compartments and the return to open-plan coaches. Compartments compartmentalise, enclose people mentally as well as physically. Open coaches open people out and at least give us an illusion of greater freedom – as long as 'They' do not seal them with hermetic tinted glass.

M. cannot understand how I can arrive at Paddington half an hour early for a train. Suspect she thinks me mad. I just enjoy being in Brunel's cathedral. Like its religious counterparts, the station has, as well as echoing aisles and transepts, all manner of squints and slypes, plaques and memorials, metalwork and woodcarving, mysterious doors and stairways, bookstalls and hymnboards, even an intoning cantor. *Si monumentum requiris* – Sir, come, spy, see. Wren receives due homage. Brunel little beyond an inconspicuous wall-tablet. A religious nation would show more appreciation of its secular temples. As it is, being unbelievers, we concentrate on preserving churches, relics of our Christian past, while we treat functional masterpieces as disposable. One day 'They' will destroy Paddington as 'They' have Oxford Station. While it lasts I will savour it. I could never have commuted to Euston.

At least Paddington escapes the heavy price paid by St Paul's or any other place praised in guidebooks – tourism. Foreign visitors and British travellers alike hurry through, because no one has suggested to them that they should stop and look. Organise conducted tours and charge admission – as they do so shamefully at Westminster Abbey – and you would have queues stretching down Praed Street to the Edgware Road.

Siderodromology: the study of railways.

ANTI-KONTAKION 14

*A curse on the train. Defecating freak. Micturating masto-
don. Incontinent container. Untrained train. Fouler of its own fair-
way. Polluter. Contaminator. Commuter-exterminator.* Anathema
sit.

Women's Liberation, Gay Liberation, Black Liberation,
Palestine Liberation, Symbionese Liberation, even Animal
Liberation. But Commuter Liberation. . .? Huh.

Lines of quite modern coaches discarded near Didcot. Each
one with an easily overlooked COND stencilled in a corner.
COND, not just quietly to rust and decay, but to have their
dissolution hastened by vandals with stones. Only a wire
mesh fence separates their lazaretto from the compound,
Abraham's bosom, where enthusiasts labour to rescue more
ancient rolling-stock. Too old to be white hopes and blue-
eyed prospects, too young to be worth preserving as relics,
we feel a sympathetic pang as we trundle past the betrayed
carriages – COND and conned.

Strange that my first long book (unpublished) – *In Which
Our Hero Sets Forth* – took the form of a railway journey from
Oxford to Paddington. I wrote it in Greece and Cornwall,
stuffing it with autobiographical digressions which prolifer-
ated as I realised more and more how much of my past
impinged upon those sixty miles of track.

I had too much time in those days. Today I have too
little. Commuterdom, which I then so insolently spurned, is
enjoying its revenge. Hundreds of times a year, like a guilty
dog, muzzle pressed into its own vomit, I retrace in
captivity what I once fondly saw as a ride towards freedom.
O irony! But I refuse to submit, and continue to follow
Carlyle's advice to 'sit still and label [my] thoughts'.

Cecil Day-Lewis read *In Which Our Hero Sets Forh* for
Chatto and Windus. He commented that I might one day
make a travel-writer. Clearly an oracular pronouncement –
Delphi clings to the slopes of Parnassus. Like the best

Sibylline utterances, it is coming true in an unforeseen, ambiguous manner. Ten years ago, when I wrote *Our Hero*, I erred in going through the motions of throwing off a restraint I had never known. Since then I have gained first-hand experience of the coffle. Now, a chastened anti-hero, I can set forth in lively earnest.

'Travel' is cognate with 'travail'. Both descend from medieval Latin *trepalium*, a three-pronged instrument of torture. No wonder 'They' have done 'Their' best to expunge the classics from the syllabus.

Notebook constitutes alexipharmic, amulet, apotropaic, demonifuge, phylactery, prophylactic, talisman, against that sense of futility which prompts many more books than those which treat of it explicitly. I scribble and jot in hope that I have found a valid way of redeeming the time. But how to be sure?

The Unquiet Grave a masterpiece, but Palinurus himself a risky guide. He might steer me on to rocks and shoals.

Greeting between Oxford station staff – accents broad, understanding perfect: 'Morning, Arthur.' 'Mornin', Abdul.'

LOOSE COUPLING 8

'Streetly between oursells,' said she,
'I shall say what I feel,
So tell me what that mole's for, dear?'
'For added sex appeal,'
Replied he; she did cotton on
And cried: 'I shall not give
An apple for decorum now,
However long I live!'

I used to admire among the regulars a small, plump, middle-aged Asian. In morning he would savage the *Financial Times*, leaving most of it in shreds on floor, inserting a few choice scraps in a large bulldog clip. In evening, his business evidently satisfactorily discharged, he would sip brandy and meditate with Buddhist serenity. More recently, however, he has appeared shrunken and preoccupied. At night now he lines up two or three miniature brandies, downs them hastily, and waxes maudlin and morose. His ancient eyes are far from gay. Witnessing his transformation from contemplative Oriental to harassed Westerner, I worry not only for him, but for us all. When miners, deep beneath the surface, see their caged canary gasping for breath, they know it's time to get the hell out.

M. sometimes edits tapes on the train. Once I travelled in a full compartment where a man sat in a corner unconcernedly using a dictaphone as he went through his correspondence, complete with Borgean oral punctuation. One of his replies concerned the dismissal of an employee for unsatisfactory work. He seemed too thick-skinned to consider either that we might know the unfortunate whom he was firing, or that we might not wish to be privy to his post-bag. A dictaphone or tape-recorder certainly circumvents train-jog (though does it not pick up extraneous sounds?), but I cannot visualise myself, even in an empty compartment, solemnly or otherwise dictating these notes. Like the little girl, I need to see what I say before I can know what I think.

Have compared writing Notebook to Agag-like walk on sleepers. Yes, but process also resembles constructing a railway. Roger the Navigator. Varied terrain makes rate of progress uncertain. No contract, no schedule, simply a vague sense of urgency. No plans even, no blueprint. Every time I down tools I have advanced the railhead a little further into *terra incognita*. No way to build a railroad, but the best a loner can manage. I have finished, yet I have not started. I do not know the location or the nature of the terminus, yet I have already arrived. Where I leave off, the exposed rail-ends reach to infinity.

Man, seeing me looking out of window, offers me the *Daily Telegraph*, inquiring: 'Do you want to pollute yourself with this?'

Arouses the pedant in me – not difficult! – when announcers refer to 'the seventeen hundred train'. Do they seriously believe each day has two thousand four hundred hours? When they apologise for 'the delayed eighteen hundred', will no one tell them that Queen Anne and Queen Victoria are dead? But I like 'the eighteen twelve' which I think of as the Cannon Ball Express. The 1605 should go like a bomb. A rebellious lot travel on the 1715. You risk suffocation on the 1756. As for the 1815 – why Paddington?

The Great Train of Being: a theory in vogue for about a hundred years between 1850 and 1950. It proposed dividing human beings into three classes, further subdivided into compartments, sometimes intercommunicating, sometimes not. It further suggested that these categorised people might, to everyone's benefit, be conveyed long distances along pre-ordained routes. This theory has now been totally discredited.

S., a short girl, complains that all seats in new coaches are standard size geared to people about six feet tall. Suggests seating graded to suit various heights, or no seating at all. She observes: 'Sitting is an unnatural position. The Chinese, who squat, do not suffer from arthritis.' All the same, I doubt if they squat on trains. They probably have more sense than to travel on them, and stay at home instead sticking needles into themselves to prevent arthritis. Japanese, on other hand, when not on kamikaze missions in bullet-trains, attempt hara-kiri on their underground system where students spend their vacations practising the martial art of compressing commuters. The whole world needs Red Guards to destroy its tyrannical trains.

On our sixty-mile trip we do not encounter a single tunnel. We go over and under various bridges. At Ealing Broadway 'They' have boxed in two stretches of track with reinforced girders on top of which 'They' have placed buildings. I hope that these soon collapse – preferably without loss of life – to discourage 'Them' from encasing all railways everywhere in concrete waistcoats. Some of the bridges have stalactites hanging from them. Have noticed on sunny days, if I have eyes shut as train flashes under a bridge, I see for a moment a vivid, almost tangible, electric blue light.

We pass over and under old bridges, new bridges, high bridges, low bridges, metal, wooden, concrete, stone, and brick bridges, footbridges, road bridges, bridges over water (no aqueducts), bridges over railways, bridges built by Brunel, anonymous sleepy bridges for farm animals, canopied station bridges, flat bridges, arched bridges, decaying stumps of amputated bridges.

Just outside Paddington we also pass beneath the great new road to the west. Hardly a bridge as such – ponderous concrete segments supported by colossal piers, the whole giving an impression of great weight and great lightness like a swan in flight, with the sinuosity of a swan's neck too. Beautiful engineering that Brunel might admire. We, seeing it from underneath as it curves away on either side, cutting a serpentine swathe through the tenements, can appreciate its aesthetic qualities better than those who drive along it. The road-users, by way of compensation, enjoy an aerial view of the railway tracks and the trains. Over and under, under and over – so much depends on perspective.

I always carry a string of Greek worry-beads for use in an emergency.

Why did we call the little Abingdon train 'the bunk'? (G., of an older generation, knew it as 'the bumper'.) At Radley now 'They' have nailed sheets of metal over the words FOR ABINGDON. The branch-line quietly rusts.

Have known trains cancelled because of 'carriage shortage' or 'locomotive shortage'. What happens? Do they suddenly run out like a housewife's supplies of sugar and bread? Do entrepreneurs hoard rolling-stock in secret sheds, waiting for the price to rise? A possible clue: a plaque fixed to sides of some engines declares 'This Locomotive Is The Property Of English Electric Leasings Ltd'. It recalls similarly labelled hotel towels and coat-hangers. Surprising to find that British Rail do not own all their engines. The warning notice implies that, like the Ritz and the Seaview Guest House, English Electric Leasings suffer from thievery – true train robbery – whence the periodic shortages.

ANTI-KONTAKION 15

A curse on the train. Living death. Dying life. Chapel of unease. Coffle of disease. Hearse conveying the living to a hurried grave. Coffin containing the dying buried alive. Anathema sit.

Our trains reserve no seats for those in special need – *femmes enceintes* and the rest. Perhaps 'They' realise that every commuter has some debility that would qualify him for preferential treatment. *Nous, les mutilés de gare.* Seats marked 'For The Use Of The Hale And Hearty Only' would, more often than not, remain unoccupied.

TRACKSIDE INDUSTRY 5

Alf Meade, meat importer, owner of a fleet of refrigerated pantechnica. Most of the wagons just have his name and trade on the side, but one or two uncompromisingly declare: 'You must succeed with meat from Meade' – a throwback to the Victorian and Edwardian heyday of advertising, before the Trades Description Act spoiled the fun. Succeed in what way? At what? To what? Idle to speculate. One could try consuming a leg of mutton from Mr Meade, but how to know for certain that any subsequent success was propter *and not merely* post hock*?*

Department of irrelevant coincidence: Shepherd Mead wrote How to Succeed in Business without Really Trying. *The book succeeded, and Mead retired at the age of 41 to write several sequels. Cannot see how to work in* Coming of Age in Samoa, *except to say that: You must succeed with a name like Mead.*

My briefcase bulges because it contains, among other things, several notebooks and a five-year diary. But when, from time to time, people ask me what I carry to and fro, remembering *Arms and the Man*, I reply 'chocolate creams'. You can always tell an old commuter by the inside of his briefcase. The young ones carry business correspondence and pocket calculators: the old ones mental anaesthetics and grub.

Everything flows. Heracleitus's dictum has never been refuted. It appeals to the commuter, but could mislead. To appreciate the true flow of things one needs to stand still. The apparent flow of landscape past the train windows deludes us. The movement of the train cozens us. The train cannot move any faster than that oak tree in the field over there – its wheels spin in the grit of time.

Even so, motion has genuine compensations. We view hills, woods, buildings, clouds, as if visitors to a sculpture exhibition. I have heard several commuters remark on the beauty of the rounded hill beside Cholsey. Half its attraction for us lies in the fact that we see it *while moving*. Transported rapidly past it, we obtain an impression of its shape, its contours, its essence, not vouchsafed to a static observer.

This principle especially effective with the factoryscape nearer London. Seen in full sunshine from speeding train, drabness and ugliness become transfigured. Sharp silhouettes, planes, shadows, angles, shapes, masses, reflections, loom, strike, shift, wax large, diminish – silently and very fast. Kinetic excitement.

LOOSE COUPLING 9

'When girls ask me to cull 'em, I
Do not think of them badly,'
He said; and she: 'I was afeerd
I'd acted rather addly.'

Buffet-car attendants, ticket-collectors, guards – minor Shakespearian characters. Some scarcely noticed. Others, making the most of their walk-on parts, threatening to steal the show. The train provides a stage. But, thank God, all the world is *not* a train.

LITERARY LANDMARK 6, MAIDENHEAD

Maidenhead is not a literary landmark. It ought to be.

On one side of coach a warning sign: No Smoking Maximum Penalty £25; on the other: Maximum Penalty £10; elsewhere only £5. Inhalation struggling to keep up with inflation.

(Stop Press: Since I wrote this note, a year or two back, the fine has increased to £50.)

Slavery has been abolished, but the laws of emancipation do not touch us as we toil away in the train-gang. Few can afford to buy their way out. Few, anyway, have sufficient energy or initiative left to discover – not easy this – either the price of freedom or to whom one should pay it. Hebetude holds us.

Palinurus quotes John Donne:

We are all conceived in close prison . . . and then all our life is but a going out to the place of execution, to death. Nor was there any man seen to sleep in the cart between Newgate and Tyburn – between prison and the place of execution, does any man sleep? But we sleep all the way; from the womb to the grave we are never thoroughly awake.

O Notebook, in you repose my hopes of manumission. To you I cling as to an altar of asylum. Do not let the tumbril bear me away.

Pascal attributed man's troubles to his inability to stay put in one room. On the contrary, man suffers from claustrophilia: cf. De Selby, who ascribed 'the softening and degeneration of the human race . . . to its progressive predilection for interiors and waning interest in the art of going out and staying there'. We skulk in houses, motor cars, trains, incubating unhealthy schemes, when we would do far better to expose ourselves to the elements as Lear did. King or Edward? Take your pick. Both lived on or over the verge of madness. Both turned to cryptic language and rugged nature in their search for salvation. Commuters especially need to abjure all roofs and to heed the warning of Uncle Arly's Railway Ticket.

Notes to the Hurrying Man (Patten). Notes from, for, by the hurrying man (Tiresias). There is a book who runs may read. Ay, and another who commutes may write.

Salvation lies in going off the rails – both in leaving them and in becoming disillusioned with them. Only machines, automata, come to grief if they leave the rails. Human beings who do so discover the fruitful joys of a little insanity and start to live. (See *Zorba passim*.)

We old-stagers can instantly recognise our whereabouts not only with our eyes open, but with them shut too. We subconsciously register every change of speed, every cambered bend, every clattering stretch of old track, every swishing bridge, reverberant cutting or resonant station. Even the nose comes into play from time to time as we pick up such scents as sewage, burning rubber, or, in season, stubble fires and mustard fields.

More trucks with ungainly names: Palvan Shock, Covhop, Flatrol, Merdog, Pasfruit, Presflo, Shockhood, Vanwide, Lowmac, Palvan, Match, Shocbar, Borail, Polybulk, Fährbootwagen.

More trucks with the functional names: Creosote, China Clay Only, Orehop, Timber, Newspaper Packing Van, Beer, Soda Ash, Clay Hood, Gunpowder, Ash.

More rolling-stock which defies categorisation: Electrification, Stores Van, Trestle, Cell Truck, Weed Control Services, Coil, Ale Pallet, Inter-City Exhibition Train, Weight Wagon, Track Recording Unit, Hy-Mac Equipment, Safety Train, High Cradle, Bridge Dept, Barrier Wagon, Roller Wagon, Winch Wagon, Universal Viaduct Inspection Unit, Independent Snowplough.

More legends on rolling-stock: This Set To Be Marshalled At Front Of Train, Buckeye Ex, Dangerous Traffic, Brake Isolating Cock, Engineering Dept For The Conveyance Of Long Welded Rails Only, Wagon Not To Travel With Hood Open, Do Not Load Or Move, Danger Keep Clear

When Lifting Or Lowering Shoulders, Not To Be Loaded With Fish, For Use On Weed Killing Train, Not In Common Use, Hopper Doors Must Be Closed Before Wagon Is Moved, Door Pins Greasing Due.

Dear Notebook, can I ask you for a moment to take on a new role, that of confidant or confessional? Just like everybody's image of the harassed commuter, I went to the office party and spent five hours trading kisses with a beautiful girl whose precocious father I could just about be. Typically sordid? To me it seemed neither typical nor sordid. Inevitable, complete, without hope. It concerns you, O Notebook, because the episode fills my mind as I trundle to and fro. The pounding train drives home the sweetly despairing words she murmured in my ear: 'But you have a wife and two children, a wife and two children, a wife and two children. . .' Ah, the perils of working sixty miles from home, of being a daily *Gastarbeiter*!

ANTI-KONTAKION 16
A curse on the train. Type of man's downfall in the Genesis story. Serpent seductively sliding, a tempting devil. Tree of the knowledge of good and evil. Flaming sword barring our return to happiness. Garment of fig-leaves wrapping our nakedness. Anathema sit.

Like boxers we enter the ring in the hope of carrying off huge purses. Like most boxers most of us will end our days in punch-drunk penury. We know this, yet fondly imagine some strange virtue lies in taking our punishment, in refusing to go down for the count. At weekends we slump in our corners for the too short intervals between rounds with damp towels and painkillers before the battering begins again. Ding, ding! Wives out of the ring. We can only win by withdrawing from the contest, by denying the yelling fans their blood.

LOOSE COUPLING 10
'A pox for decency,' exclaimed
The trouser-buttoning swain;

> *'I'll second that,' the lass rejoined,*
> *'I'm glad I caught this train!'*

Buffers

Some days the ticket-inspectors work the coach in tandem, taking alternate sides or tables or compartments, like pairs of priests administering a profane communion, false hierophants.

Why do 'They' retain absurd distinction between First and Second Class? Far more helpful if 'They' divided us into, say, talkers and non-talkers, or farters and non-farters. Seriously.

Have yet to spot on our line an example of the legendary practice of affixing a card to yourself saying: 'Wake Me At Oxford'. Hope I never do. But we do go so far as to lay our season tickets face upwards on the table before we drop off. An old shikari's trick.

Oxford Station staff use tannoy not only for communicating with public, but also for sending one another messages like: 'Clock down your end one minute slow, George', 'One lady in a blue coat coming over for Kingham', 'Still two minutes to go, Ginge, old friend', 'Take your hands out of your pockets', and 'Moon's still shining' (it wasn't). An element of humour and humanity unknown at Didcot, Reading, or Paddington.

OVERHEARD 5

Donnish type with chaotic papers on knee to younger ditto: 'Droog – it's ancient Persian. English, you see, has no word for a thoroughly poisonous, evil fellow.'

For some time Paddington had an announcer who invariably used the construction: 'The 1659 train to Reading are the first six coaches at Platform 7.' Mentioned this to

A., saying: 'I'm sure there's a grammatical term for this.' 'Yes,' he replied laconically, 'wrong.'

For every passenger on the 1715 who reads *The Field*, there is one on the 1815 who reads *Private Eye*.

That train again! (Shakeliver)

OVERHEARD 6
Commuter at Paddington to non-commuting friend who had saved him a seat: 'I'm sorry, can we go on the right-hand side? Port out, starboard home, you know.'

COMMUTER'S CALENDAR 3
24 June: Heat. Haymaking. Holidaymakers.

Prowling round Paddington again. Vast, featureless, seldom-visited side like a Salonica tobacco warehouse. Inconspicuous door marked: Chief Engineer's Plan Mounting Section. What does he do in there? Frame old maps in passe-partout? Plot ingenious new ways of delaying trains? Nothing?

Nearby, another door with a sign: HQ Club, British Rail Staff Dining Club. This appears to lead to same place as door inside station labelled: Paddington (Passenger) Dining Club, Staff and Tradesmens (*sic*) Entrance Only. How to reconcile the two? Do members ever take luncheon? Could '(Passenger)' mean 'staff who work on passenger trains'? If so, is there class-distinction between these and goods staff? Perhaps the whole thing is an elaborate front, a master-plan mounted by the Chief Engineer to baffle the *profanum vulgus*. Will J.B. please contact M as soon as possible?

ALTERNATIVE TITLE 1
What Did You See On The Train, Daddy?

Fellow-victims: a hamper of live sea-anemones in transit from Plymouth to Oxford University Zoology Dept; a cardboard box labelled: Live Reptiles – will die if delayed; another marked: Alive Plants – Please Rush.

II

My words will hardly express my meaning,
But if I say that we left Paddington
At ten minutes past nine and that now
The time is a quarter past twelve,
That will be an approximation,
An inadequate attempt to convey my message
To the Minister for Transport and to
All whose business has to do with trains, and
Those concerned with every awful traffic
And those who conduct them.
The battered caravan creaks, groans, then
Lurches lethargically into the tail of the night.
The wheels have not time for many revolutions,
Stridently screaming in protestation
Against the absurd effort of motion,
For presently the train arrives in the station –
I have been here before too.

Like teenagers hardened in discos, we become impervious to the constant background of train *noise*. We talk over it, sleep through it, meditate to its accompaniment. Yet all the time its decibels conduct their assault like jungle drums.

Similarly we disregard train *smell*. While noise penetrates our brains, diesel fumes infiltrate our bodies. Unlike Mithridates, we cannot regulate the amount of daily damage to our systems. We grow oblivious but not immune.

> Slowly the poison the whole bloodstream fills,
> The waste remains, the waste remains and kills.
> (Empson)

People claim to have discovered in the Bible references to space-ships and visitors from other planets, or to have found evidence that Stonehenge was a launching-pad for prehistoric rockets. If such theories contain a grain of truth, how much more probable that old civilisations also knew what we consider the more standard trappings of an industrial society. Take ancient Greece. Acropolises were clearly sited on high hills to facilitate landing and take-off of helicopters. Santorini alias Atlantis was a base for submarines. Delphi a centre for motor-cycle races. Olympia a racing-car circuit. Most obvious of all, Knossos was the grandest railway terminus the world has ever known. Daedalus invented the steam engine and laid out a labyrinthine system linking the hundred cities of Crete. No wonder his puffing locomotives gave rise to legends of snorting, taurine monsters. See my forthcoming work: *Linear B, a Minoan Bradshaw*.

Commuting gives us one-track minds – the track between Oxford and Paddington. Only occasionally do we remember that British Rail (Western Region), though no longer Great, still serves places like Cardiff, Swansea, Bristol, Worcester, Hereford, Exeter, Plymouth. cf. E.M. Forster, *Howards End*: 'In Paddington all Cornwall is latent and the remoter west.' When something reminds me, I long to leap aboard the next train for Penzance, never to return. To settle in Mousehole among daffodils and granite boulders. To exchange the noise and smell of the train for those of the Atlantic. Cannot think of one good reason why I have not done this. And yet . . . And yet . . .

Two examples of sadism. i. Morning at Didcot. 0700 from Oxford pulls in. Passengers disembark to wait at another platform for a faster train to London. When they have entered subway, announcer proclaims that fast train has been cancelled. They all turn back. At same time 0700 moves quietly off, leaving them neatly stranded.

ii. Evening, somewhere around Tilehurst. Weary commuters sleep, read, or stare blankly. Suddenly a buffet attendant, who clearly prides himself on being a bit of a one, flings open door at end of coach, shouting: 'Anyone for Didcot or Swindon?' Sheepish hands go up. He takes a long look before declaring: 'Well, you're on the right train, ha ha ha ha!'

Like birds and animals, we seldom collapse or die in public. When we feel our time drawing near, we creep quietly home to our burrows. We must avoid unpleasantness on the train at all costs.

Once 'They' distributed copies of a questionnaire inviting us to suggest improvements to the service. (We did our best, telling 'Them' that we should like more trains to stop at Hanwell and Elthorne, and that we wanted coaches fitted out as a sauna, a gymnasium and a reference library.) At other times 'They' have issued the ticket-inspectors with dictaphones into which they mutter: 'One annual season Kingham to Moorgate, one reduced pensioner, one corn-flakes special offer, one day-return, one awayday golden rail winterbreak bargain, one living corpse, one sex maniac,' and so on. No doubt 'They' file all this information away somewhere. (Perhaps it goes to the Chief Engineer's Plan Mounting Section.) Such surveys never have any results that we can detect.

Someone – not 'They' for it would be against 'Their' interests – should be conducting a different kind of research, on the effects of commuting on the human metabolism. They should strap monkeys into trains, wire them up to all manner of instruments, shoot them into orbit between Oxford and Paddington, and monitor their reactions. I doubt if any monkey would survive such treatment for more than a few days. They would soon succumb to swollen ankles, shaken livers, piles, back-pains, headaches, dizziness, nausea, deafness, lung cancer, *delirium trainens*, and general nervous depression. Animal-lovers would hold demonstrations. Letters of protest would appear in the newspapers. Questions would be asked in the House. The experiment would prove what we all know already, but are reluctant to face up to – that every coach should carry the message: Warning by H.M. Government, Commuting Can Damage Your Health.

ANTI-KONTAKION 17
A curse on the train. Ship to Tarshish. Trip to Tartarus. Death Row. Breath's foe. Theatre of the absurd. Theatre of cruelty. Haunt hateful to fauna. Habitat hostile to flora. Anathema sit.

People from Malvern, Hereford, South Wales, so much more friendly, easygoing and relaxed than us. For them the worlds of *Piers Plowman*, Kilvert's Diaries, and *Under Milk Wood* still exist. We ask them: 'What's the smell of parsley?' We, the forgetting and forgotten in our world whose texts are *The Castle, The Inferno, Huis Clos, 1984*. Works written by commuters of the soul.

'Will the mechanical foreman please ring 2251.' Now we *know*.

TRACKSIDE INDUSTRY 6
Outside a factory near Langley, several carefully lettered notices: No Off Loading Unless Company Personell Present.

Concentration of Gunpowder wagons at Didcot. Build-up of MoD (Army) rolling-stock at Reading with tanks, guns and armoured cars. Can't wait for the day when we wake to martial music on the radio and announcements that the railway has been blown up, that citizens should remain calmly in their homes, that peace and normality prevail.

To my surprise and consternation, I find myself entering into possession of the railway, beginning to make the train my own. Unwelcome gift. Watching, on television, Lawrence Durrell in Corfu and Rhodes, I thought: 'My God, if I become famous I shall have to do films about commuting instead of about my beloved Greece. O the dangers of annexing the wrong province!'

Two things comfort me. One: the unlikelihood of fame. Two: the recollection that Durrell started by chronicling the English Death from which he then escaped. Imagine lecturing to Women's Institutes on the Oxford to Paddington grind! Imagine howling: 'tis too horrible!

ALTERNATIVE TITLE 2
Between the Lines.

Tried to quiz J., a steam fanatic, on the origins of truck-names. But he babbled of Crocodiles, Macaws and ten-ton

Toads. Minnows and Mermaids too modern for him. Pleasure, on other hand, at discovering in A. a fellow-truck-fancier. His wife S. – also a commuter – disapproved of our swapping of Prawns and Bolsters. Not done in polite society to bandy esoteric terms.

The Unquiet Grave forty years on. Palinurus's world, his ethos, have vanished as surely as my train-world will, thank God, vanish – is already vanishing. Palinurus sought to exorcise angst through writing. Today, the angst is the message. Tomorrow, the bicycle races and rejoicing.

Occasional regulars who drop in on us when not flying to Basel, Teheran, Washington, Johannesburg, Sydney, or attending conferences in Scunthorpe and Bognor Regis. They derive reassurance from finding us still *in situ* when they return. They smile at us, speak to us, treat us like human beings; but they do not really understand our predicament. They cannot – and why should they? – narrow their broad horizons down to our restricted compass. We sense so strongly the barrier they fail to perceive. Fair-weather trippers who use the train like a holiday resort, and see us as picturesque locals, the *longueurs* of whose bitter, inward-looking winters they will never know or even suspect.

As the years pass, the process grows grimmer. Ages since the last black velvet party, and that an abortive one when F., the celebrant, missed the train. Few these days make the successful dash across the tracks, over or under the perimeter fence to freedom. No more crossing-the-line ceremonies. No more carefree camaraderie. We who remain have no illusions left. The goodyears shall devour us.

Near Slough one day, a van marked: Immediate Transportation Co. Curious how a word which once denoted a dreaded punishment now signifies a sought-after service. Not for us, though. Condemned to do the flitting of the bat. Sentenced to transportation for life. Even eighteenth-century sheep-stealers had a better prospect than ours in the chance of a new antipodean life. We have no Tasmania in view. For us the actual process of transportation never ceases. No landfall, however distant, awaits us.

Our fate more analogous to that of galley-slaves, conditioned to row mindlessly in a windowless hold. The state conscripts us to serve in its galley-trains which without us could not run. Without us they would lose their *raison d'être*. What a staggering, yet simple truth: commuters exist solely to keep the trains going. Yet we fondly persist in believing that trains exist to keep *us* going. Through propaganda and other techniques 'They' have hypnotised us into supposing ourselves shackled to oars and duty-bound to row. 'They' count on our lacking the will-power to shatter this illusory image, to pass through the barrier one night never to return.

Anyone who, like myself, having reached the stage on the path of enlightenment where he realises the utter irrelevance and superfluity of the train, does not forsake it immediately, is certifiably insane. The cure: an intensive, Coué-like course of repetition of this rune: 'I do not need the train. I do *not* need the train. I do NOT need the train.'

COMMUTER'S CALENDAR 4
1 July: Drought. Dog Daisies.

Call me Jonah. I have disobeyed the inner voice. I went down to the station; I found a train going to Paddington: I paid the fare thereof, and went down into it, to go with them unto Paddington from the presence of the Lord. Throw me overboard to stop the daily wreck of lives. Let me be born again in the amniotic peace of the fish's belly.

Ship-train = man-made symbol of disobedience and death.

Sojourn in whale = return to life-giving nature, regeneration.

MYSTERY 13
Did I dream Paddington announcer calling for 'the water dowser'?

Sheep/goat distinction not entirely accurate. Some commuters show alarmingly ovine tendencies, e.g. those who, as far out as Ealing Broadway, start to flock to the front of the train. They cram the corridor of the first coach, fondly supposing that this manoeuvre will help them to reach their desks more quickly. In fact, the congestion caused by their stampede ensures that most of them gain nothing over those who disembark at their leisure further down the train.

They never learn, even though the train's pauses outside Paddington in the morning, and Oxford in the evening, often make them suffer discomfort and frustration. An awful compulsion possesses them. A lady from Didcot confessed to me one day: 'Really it doesn't matter what time I get to the office, but I can't stop myself getting up and hurrying to the front of the train.' Hey, ho, Didcot dame! Hey, ho, seely sheepe!

COMMUTER'S CALENDAR 5
8 July: Watery Welkin. Willowherb. Whin. Waving Wheat. Wet Warmth. Wind-tossed Willows.

Despite impressions to contrary, train seldom comes to complete standstill. The rare pleasure of being stationary, of having the opportunity closely to con a few yards of track or verge. To count pebbles. To study flowers and grasses. To note cryptic inscriptions, such as this one chalked on side of a rail: M.H.3′6″ BELOW THIS RAIL. A grave? A mousehole? What?

COMMUTER'S CALENDAR 6
16 July: Harvest. Horse-chestnuts. Heraldic Heron in Hayfield.

ANTI-KONTAKION 18
A curse on the train. Endless transportation of convicts. Condemnation to galleys for conscripts. Self-sought slavery. Self-bought captivity. Placer round wrists of invisible chains. Holder in thrall of our risible brains. Anathema sit.

Writing a Premeditated Notebook a slow, difficult process. Easier to toss off continuous prose. You cannot write too many items at a sitting. Entries need space between them. Yes, and also time. The reader cannot discern this separating time, but he can sense its absence. Advantage for writer and reader: either can pick up or break off at any point. The form encourages both to pause, reflect, browse in other books; and also takes in its stride persons from Porlock.

ALTERNATIVE TITLE 3
The Unquiet Train.

'They' have long since discontinued Pullman cars. No point in sumptuous fittings for the cells in Death Row.

Dear Notebook, you constitute my act of Dodgsonism – a gage which I fling defiantly on to the track.

Travel broadens the mind. Commuting narrows it.

'A buffet car will be conveyed on this train' always sounds odd. Why? The train conveys people and goods in its rolling-stock. It does not convey the rolling-stock. The train *is* the rolling-stock. More correct: 'This train includes a buffet car.' Most correct: 'The usual collection of regular old soaks will be conveyed in the buffet car.' Gratuitous note: the etymology of 'buffet' in this sense is unknown.

After looking at some critics on Auden's *Journal of an Airman*, I begin modestly to suspect myself the first to realise that works like this constitute a distinct literary genre. The first to isolate the bacillus of the Premeditated Notebook.

COMMUTER'S CALENDAR 7
28 July: Brazen Brightness. Blond Bales. Burnt Berks and Bucks. Bleached Boeotian Bone.

Imprisoned in every fat man a thin one is wildly signalling to be let out (Palinurus). Imprisoned in every commuter moulders a human being who, even though he may have ceased to signal, could yet be released, if only . . .

114

(Poignantly Ambiguous) HEADLINE 5
Reading Man Killed By Car.

Chamberlain says: Beware of the meticulous man who reads the *Financial Times* folded into precise quarters.

A note on perspective. Am almost overcome by sense of outrage when someone lights up near me in No Smoking compartment; yet, if obliged to sit where smoking is permitted, I bask happily in the fumes, taking a trip on other people's nicotine. Why? Why should a label on a window alter my attitude? I try to appear defiant, rebellious. I kid myself that I *am* a rebel. But confront me with a notice, an announcement, an instruction, a convention even, and I crack at once, submit without a struggle, conform unquestioningly.

No need for 'Them' to worry about me. 'They' have me where 'They' want me. So subtly conditioned that I can no longer tell freedom from bondage. Must combat 'Them' by constant effort to become less crotchety, less respectable, less apoplectic, more open, more accepting, more tolerant, more loving. Yet how to be sure that to take even such a course is not to play into 'Their' hands? 'Their' subtlety and cunning know no limits.

Said I saw Notebook as an astronaut's log. But perhaps it is my space-ship. After a long wait on the pad and an interrupted countdown, we have blasted off. The train, our launching-gantry, fell away and disintegrated as we rose. Now we are cruising in space at a speed of 10,000 words per year, on a voyage that may last a lustrum or more. Beauty and monotony have kissed each other, and from their union spring interstellar confidence, galactic hope.

HEADLINE 6
Mermaid In High Banana Shock.

Didcot a good place for Railways, Rabbits, Ragwort, Rosebay willowherb.

ALTERNATIVE TITLE 4
The London Nod.

Life does not separate the frivolous and the serious. Nor do I. I intend Notebook as a bomb with built-in anti-handling devices. Attempt to dismantle it at your peril. Tug any one sentence too roughly and the whole lot will explode in your mind.

OVERHEARD 7
'Will you behave? You're frightening the birdie and it's not nice.' Mother to small boy. On table between them a huge birdcage, empty except for small, silent receptacle on floor, labelled: Bird Carrying Box.

Laying it on a bit thick: 'Light refreshments only will be served on the 1700 tonight. We apologise for all the inconvenience this will cause.'

Laying it on a bit thin: 'We apologise for the delay, which was due to a slight technical fault.'

ANTI-KONTAKION 19
A curse on the train. Receiver coffering men's aspirations. Deceiver offering false revelations. Great train of being – an illusory notion. Imparter to landscape of delusory motion. Anathema sit.

The end of the line – where life begins.

A Rune for the extremely jaded: 'It was one of those overcast, brooding daybreaks with a menacing yellow tinge, like the interior of a modern train.'

Didcot porter, asked about next train for Oxford, points to train waiting to leave and says: 'This is Oxford.' (See my forthcoming article: The Limits of Synecdoche.)

Beginning to realise that Palinurus had something with his wistful hankering after girls he had never met. He extracted a lot of mileage from harmless speculation. Masochistic pleasure. I have overstepped the boundaries of literary

116

device by embracing flesh and blood. I know now what Coventry Patmore meant:

> He that but once too nearly hears
> The music of forfended spheres
> Is thenceforth lonely, and for all
> His days like one who treads the Wall
> Of China, and on this side sees
> Cities and their civilities
> And on the other lions.

'But you have a wife and two children . . .'

Autumn has become unfashionable. People speak of the end of summer and the beginning of winter, as though nothing intervened. Commuters, however, know that autumn has come when they see Christmas cards on the move and when they glimpse, through early mist outside Oxford Station, congregating like migrating swallows, red and silver London Transport underground trains.

One of many similar graffiti on trains and stations. Never written, always scratched in uncomfortable, sharp capitals:

LASER   MURDER
RAYS   THROUGH
BODY   WALLS
PAINS   DAY AND
RED MASS   NIGHT

A tempting theory. But 'They' direct subtler secret weapons against us.

LITERARY LANDMARK 7, SLOUGH

Slough is a literary landmark. It ought not to be. Yet it does not earn its place in this series only on the strength of Sir John Betjeman's indictment:

> Come, friendly bombs, and fall on Slough,
> It isn't fit for humans now,
> There isn't grass to graze a cow,
> Swarm over, Death!

Betjeman could more appositely have written: 'No yard of soil left to plough', because, as we clatter through Slough Station, we could see, two or three miles away, if it wasn't for the factories in between, Stoke Poges church, past which Thomas Gray's ploughman once wearily plodded. Gray's Elegy makes solemn reading for all, but especially for the commuter who every day participates in the madding crowd's ignoble strife.

Somewhere near Slough Station, the train bisects the path Gray used to take between Stoke Poges and Eton. Somewhere, in the middle of all this light industry, all these roads and railway lines, beneath these lumbering jumbo jets, lies the spot where the idea came to him for his Ode on a Distant Prospect of Eton College. Perhaps, oppressed by ballast and sleepers, the place is pounded hourly by a thousand flanged wheels. Gray could scarcely have predicted the soulless horror of Slough, but the Ode does contain some uncannily prophetic lines:

> Alas, regardless of their doom,
>   The little victims play!
> No sense have they of ills to come,
>   Nor care beyond today;
> Yet see how all around 'em wait
> The Ministers of human fate,
>   And black Misfortune's baleful train!

Somehow he knew. . .

COMMUTER'S CALENDAR 8

1 September: Singed Stubble. Soil-Searching Seagulls. Swallows Soon to Seek Southern Sun.

When I began Notebook, I saw myself as a chronicler of contemporary moments. (If I saw myself at all. I set out all insouciance; self-consciousness and introspection have forced their way in with the passage of time.) A Xenophon or a Tacitus. Now, rather to my surprise, I find I have become a willing Gibbon, describing a way of death which, thank God, is itself dying. Rising fares and winters of misery are doing more than this Notebook ever will to lure long-distance commuters from the strait and narrow permanent way.

Twenty-first-century scholars will read these pages with disbelief. Surely human beings of the 1970s could not voluntarily have undergone such degradation, such loss of dignity? They will subject Notebook to various tests, suspecting a hoax. Its genuineness established, they will treat the enigma of the Oxford to Paddington commuters like that of the Lost Legion. Gradually they will gather collateral evidence – a season ticket ('They' destroy most on expiry), a letter to *The Times*, an allusion in a property advertisement. They will discover how some of us died of exposure, some took our own lives, some escaped abroad, some went native, some went mad. But Notebook will provide the basis for all their research. Posterity, here we come!

Posterity my audience? Steady on! The commuter must watch himself constantly for signs of softening of the train ... True, no honest writer does not have putative readers somewhere in his mind. But for me, at present, they seem so remote that basically I am scrawling for myself alone, *in loco lectorum*. This liberates me. Unchallenged I can parade outlandish theories, coin new words, make bad puns, report conversations, compose doggerel, expose myself soul, mind and body. O Notebook, when I know you offer all this, why do I persistently neglect you?

ALTERNATIVE TITLE 5
The Coda, or The Withering of a Prose-Writer's Mind.

Mention Edward Gibbon and what happens? A perplexing portent. At Paddington, outside concourse bookshop, a table covered with cheap remainders. On examination at least half the books prove to be copies of the Revised Version of the Bible and a glossy edition of ... *The Decline and Fall of the Roman Empire*.

DIALOGUE 5
Self: 'Why is this train so late?'
Guard: 'This one come from Swansea. They said a shed got in front of the train or something.'

Self: 'A shed?'
Guard: 'That's what they said.'

Realisation that of course the Bible contains railway references. Picture Isaiah and Ezekiel in engine-sheds and everything clicks into place. 'I saw also the Lord sitting upon a throne, high and lifted up, and his train filled the temple . . . and the house was filled with smoke . . . Then flew one of the seraphims unto me, having a live coal in his hand, which he had taken with the tongs from off the altar.' (Isaiah). Ezekiel: 'A whirlwind came out of the north, a great cloud, and a fire infolding itself . . . And when the living creatures went, the wheels went by them . . . and the noise of the wheels over against them, and a noise of a great rushing . . . And it came to pass, that when he had commanded the man clothed with linen, saying, Take fire from between the wheels, from between the cherubims; that he went in, and stood beside the wheels.' Interpretation unnecessary; cf. Hercule Poirot's statement (*The Mystery of the Blue Train*): 'Trust the train . . . for it is *le bon Dieu* who drives it.' But commuter trains are driven by Apollyon.

OVERHEARD 8
Guard on 0715, impatient to leave: 'Old Tom's a bugger. 'e 'angs about waiting for passengers.'

Most difficult handwritten word I've ever deciphered up-side-down on train: palaeobotany.

John Aubrey: 'How these curiosities would be quite forgott, did not such idle fellowes as I putt them downe!'

> Who, Fear, this ghastly train can see,
> And look not madly wild, like thee?
> William Collins: *Ode to Fear*

ALTERNATIVE TITLE 6
Trains That Pass in the Day.

As Others See Us: D. told me he used to think me a lawyer – 'You have a judicial appearance.' R. said: 'I described you to my husband as a gentleman commuter.' I like that.

Have likened process of writing Notebook to building a railroad. More obviously, it resembles a railway journey with all its fits and starts, its fast smooth stretches, unexpected incidents, jerky passages etc. Sudden realisation: Notebook does not just resemble a railway journey, it is *the* railway journey. It is the track. It is the train. It is the driver, the guard, the passengers. It is me. It is all these and much more besides. It is existence. It is soul. It is metaphor pushed to the limit. It is metaphor pushed over the limit so that it becomes reality. It contains and reconciles all opposites. It is everything except God. It is my rip-cord, my *cordon sanitaire*, my green belt, my communication cord to be pulled *now*.

COMMUTER'S CALENDAR 9
12 September: Mephitic Morning Mist.

A season in hell is just the ticket.

As I travel to town, the breakfast kisses (cornflakes, milk, peanut butter) of my two small sons congeal on my cheek. Sometimes, when I come home, they clamour to know: 'What did you see from the train today, Daddy?' I rack my brains and come up with cattle, pigs, sheep, herons, boats, houses, factories, goods wagons. Nicolas and Antony turn away unsatisfied. I feel ashamed.

Henry Miller rebukes me:

Everything is so divinely connected, so beautifully interrelated – how could one possibly be at a loss to undertake the education of a child?

My feeble replies recall Sir Bedivere's:

> I heard the ripple washing in the reeds,
> And the wild water lapping on the crag.

One day, I hope, the lads will put their question, and I shall be able to hand them a completed Notebook, bound in white samite.

'British Rail regret there will be a slight delay to this train due to fitter's attention to the diesel locomotive.' Filthy fitter! Unwelcome attention!

Commuting: an unsuccessful Frankensteinian transplant operation.

No Naked Light – injunction on oil wagons. Echoes of half-remembered quotations: 'No tumbled house', 'No continuing city', 'Let no naked light come near'. It belongs to the world of Antichrist where all the best worst people hide their lights under bushels.

ANTI-KONTAKION 20
A curse on the train. Wheel of Things from which all seek salvation. Archetypal rut from which all need liberation. Divider of men into classes and carriages. Widow-maker and breaker of marriages. Anathema sit.

TRACKSIDE INDUSTRY 7
Set in old, squat, brick hut – jewel in forehead of toad – a digital clock. Underneath, a slogan: Time To Think Of Grindex Pumps. It succeeds in that it always makes me think of Grindex Pumps; but fails because, after a few seconds, I turn my mind to something else, my homage paid for another day, and the mystery as opaque as ever.

Occasional sightings of aged, bowed, bowler-hatted commuters in rusty black. Heads thrust forward on scrawny necks protruding from loose, starched collars. These shell-backs trudge along the platforms of 'mournful, ever-weeping Paddington' (Blake's prophetic phrase). They need no sandwich-boards announcing the end of the world and encouraging repentance. Their message cries out to us.

Station architecture. Oxford: nondescript hospital prefab. Didcot: Great Western traditional, *sui generis*. Reading:

stately home stables wing. Slough: municipal Bavarian with a touch of Byzantine. Langley: *hôtel de ville* – Clochemerle perhaps. Paddington: acme of the Victorian conservatory; combination of aviary, greenhouse and menagerie for monsters.

Chalk cuttings like scenery from a spaghetti western. On brink, against blue sky, black and white cat seems an outlaw watching our stagecoach pass.

TRAIN GAME 6

Finding appropriate alliterative epithets for every station. E.g.: Ozymandian Oxford. Razed Radley. Carious Culham. Aquatic Appleford. Disorganised Didcot. Chalky Cholsey. Gappy Goring. Precipitous Pangbourne. Thameside Tilehurst. Redbrick Reading. Twee Twyford. Modish Maidenhead. Tatty Taplow. Built-up Burnham. Sleazy Slough. Lubricious Langley. Invisible Iver. Water-Defended West Drayton. Half and Half Hayes and Harlington. Sikhy Southall. Hilly Hanwell. Weed-Encroached West Ealing. Electrified Beginning Ealing Broadway. Arc-lit Acton. Well Protected Westbourne Park. Right Outside Royal Oak. Pandemonian Paddington.

ALTERNATIVE TITLE 7
A Training Manual.

'Commuter'. The Greeks do not have a word for it. That shows their good sense. Commuting much more of an unimaginative Roman concept. Swedes use *pendla*, 'to swing like a pendulum'. German homosexuals wisely travel from another platform.

TRACKSIDE INDUSTRY 8

Ephemeral nature of all the undertakings we pass. No point in waxing conservationist as heavy plant supplants the plants of Sutton's Seeds. In a year or two the demolition boys will harvest the latest crop of warehouses. No one escapes. Huntley and Palmer's crumble. Mr Wall's solid blocks melt away. His Master's Voice cracks. R. Journet, purveyors of pleasing puzzles, fall victim to a giant ball-bearing run amok. Others will follow. Ladybird will fly away home.

Universal Grinders shall cease. Didcot power station will go up in smoke. Crown Cork will sink. Even Horlick's will one day wake tired . . .

Deus ex machina. The god climbs out of the machine and intervenes. *Homo in machina.* Powerless, the man remains shackled to the machine. Whether he beholds crime, accident, a fairground, a strawberry field, a golden oriole, a pub, he must pass on, he cannot stop. Cf. Mrs McGillicuddy witnessing murder in Agatha Christie's *4.50 from Paddington.*

Outside Reading one day I watched the derailment of a goods train. The trucks poured off the rails. The incident seemed to occur in another world. I felt remote and unconcerned. This state of detachment also means that we can make obscene gestures to people outside the train, or boldly ogle pretty girls, without risk of what Englishmen fear so much – involvement.

COMMUTER'S CALENDAR 10
18 September: Plovers and Pigeons Pecking behind Ploughs. Potato-Picking. Pomona Prevails.

O Notebook, my train-wave, my train-child, my train-storm in a British Rail teacup.

OVERHEARD 9
One hearty young man to another (quite unaware of double-entendre*): 'Coming for a cup of tea in the buff?'*

Some of us, as winter approaches, make a move from breezy open coaches to four-a-side fuggy compartments. From Simla to Delhi. From the mountains to the plains. See my forthcoming pamphlet: Transhumance among Commuters.

People pay high prices for old Bradshaws. Not sure why. You need much diligence and imagination to conjure from the stark figures images of steam trains and their passengers. Just as calendars show only dates, and menus merely name dishes, so timetables give nothing but times. They all have the most tenuous connection with actuality. The timetable serves as illusory backdrop to our theatre of cruelty. Smash it with your fist and peer through the hole. There lies the dark back-stage commuters' world. There lurks the Demon King.

Coach marked: Reading For Engineers Use Only. Their own travelling library?

Have nearly reached my limit of shunt.

Mosquito, fly, wasp, bee, moth, butterfly, grasshopper, even bird. All from time to time inadvertently enter the train. All immediately recognise a hostile environment and waste no time in seeking to escape. Some succeed. Some fail. All put up a fight.

Imagine if you lived in a Berkshire meadow, and suddenly found yourself in a rushing, noisy, confined space containing no green, growing thing. Eventually you extricate yourself at Paddington, and take temporary sanctuary on the one familiar object – a ragwort plant on a dirty brick wall. You live. You breathe. You give thanks. But when your initial relief has subsided, you begin to wonder whether you will ever see your meadow, your family, your friends, again. And suppose you do manage to return home. You will have suffered such disorientation, such shock, that, while to your nearest and dearest you may appear unchanged, you will never again see them with eyes of prelapsarian innocence. No wonder these involuntary winged passengers smash themselves with such frenzy against the glass.

Yet we of our own volition, we who have no wings, board the sterile train that severs us from our roots. We allow ourselves to be wrenched from our natural habitats. We talk of earning a living, supporting a family. In reality we do not need money, security, a pension any more than does a daddy-long-legs. The daddy-long-legs senses instinctively what our allegedly superior minds cannot grasp – that the train equals all the instruments of man's downfall in the Genesis story rolled into one.

The train is the Serpent seductively sliding over the rails. It is the Train of the Knowledge of Good and Evil that changes utterly all who sample its vaunted delights. It is the Flaming Sword which, flashing to and fro, bars our return to Eden. It is even the Garment of Fig-leaves in which we cower, trying to hide our shame, as the Lord God addresses us through the tannoy of our consciences.

The birds and the bees indicate the way to redemption.

COMMUTER'S CALENDAR 11
1 October: Swallows Still Swooping.

Up and down. Prepositions with extra significance – and confusion – for us because of the tradition that Oxford undergraduates go up for term and down for vacation. But you will find people in Oxford saying: 'I'm going up to Town today', and people in London declaring: 'I'm going down to Oxford for the weekend.' To the rescue comes Heracleitus. His dictum resolves the dilemma: 'the way up and the way down are one and the same'. To which we add: 'yes, and, being parallel, they never meet'.

Chalked on decaying Taplow Station: THE GHOST TRAIN STOPS HERE.

The earth hath bubbles . . . and railways have currents as rivers have. Only an anadromous few dare to swim against them.

ANTI-KONTAKION 21
A curse on the train. Somewhere. Nowhere. Rebarbative rattle. Repetitive shuttle. Hollow men's hideout. Amiens dug-out. Limiter of actions. Restricter of options. Anathema sit.

OVERHEARD 10
'I'm playing at the Bar – a little crime, the occasional divorce – I was getting into a rut in Academia.'

After six months of daylight, suddenly we have, not darkness, but artificial light. We had forgotten the variety. Neon

126

signs, winking aeroplanes, arc-lamps, street lights, head-lamps, yellow windows. Fairgrounds bristling with flashing coloured bulbs. November bonfires and fireworks. An occasional tractor ploughing at night. Fierce floodlights of stadiums. Caversham Park and Nuneham House ablaze with lights. Smoky glow of factories. Flash of welding torches. The giant chimney of Didcot power station studded with red like a paschal candle. Illuminated towers and spires of Oxford outshone by glaring filaments of the multi-storey car-park. Lightning streak of passing trains. Isolated farms transformed to bright cynosures.

Incandescence, luminescence, iridescence, fluorescence, phosphorescence. Resplendence, radiance, effulgence, brilliance. Scarcely a point along our track without some visible gleam. We had forgotten the daytime landscape contained this man-made magic, this secret message in invisible ink. Man the electrician can sit back and say: 'I limned this nightpiece, and it was my best.'

D., a weekly commuter with a *garconnière* in London as well as a wife and two children – that refrain once more – in Oxfordshire, thinks this arrangement superior to daily commuting. I consider my way of death slightly preferable. But that does not signify. When the last whistle blows, and the recording inspector asks us to surrender our tickets, both D. and I will be equally damned.

Met a man who commutes from the New Forest. Appalled him with my tales of camaraderie and conversation aboard our train. 'I've been catching the same train for years,' he said. 'I believe there are other regulars. Some chaps carry E II R briefcases, so I suppose they're civil servants. But we never *speak*.' Trappist brothers from the New Forest, we salute you!

Where did the word *Lebenstod* swim up from? I scribbled it down one day, but German-speaking friends have never heard of it. At all events a pretty accurate description of commuting.

On winter evenings, when we look at the windows, our own harassed faces stare back. A shift of focus dissolves the reflections, revealing the nocturnal world of shapes, suggestions, hints, possibilities, streaming past. Glimpses of the bottom of the pool not vouchsafed to Narcissus. Intimations of insubstantiality.

> A man who looks on glass .
> On it may stay his eye,
> Or if he pleaseth, through it pass,
> And there the heaven espy.
> (George Herbert)

At 0722 BST on 7 October 1975, the Didcot side of Appleford, I caught the sun slap bang between the Tiresian *mamelles* of Wittenham Clumps, thus:

Felt as thrilled as a Druid. It must be possible to see this phenomenon on most days from some vantage-point or other, but not so easy to get the train to coincide, on a clear morning, with the vital moment. Worth some research.

Curious that Paul Nash, who was obsessed with both Wittenham Clumps and the sun, and who loved juxtaposition, never (as far as I know) hit upon this symbol of male head on female bosom (let alone all the implications of another local name – Mother Dunch's Buttocks). He sensed that the place held a secret, but always viewed it and painted it from the same spot, a position from which the two hills appeared without the significant cleavage. Yet what does the old name Sinodun mean if not something like Breast Hill (cf. Latin *sinus*, French *sein*, and 'dune', 'down')?

Nash wrote: 'this place has a compelling magic which makes it a sympathetic setting for the occasion of the Equinox'. It would be fascinating to discover the points, on either side of the Clumps, from which, at the equinoxes, the sun appears rising and setting between the mounds. Nash's marvellous paintings of the twin mamelons, in which, with every justification, he tampers with actuality to achieve reality, have no need of scientific support. But, oddly enough, they may have it forced upon them.

Warning to theorisers: on that same day – 7/10/75 – that the sun rose between Wittenham Clumps, in the evening, seen from the same spot outside Appleford, the sun set flanked by two of the cooling towers of Didcot power station. Ergo the builders of the latter, remembering Stonehenge, had not only man-made energy but also super-human power in mind when they so carefully aligned the modern with the prehistoric. I hope that they did not neglect the prescribed sacrifices, and that they obtained favourable auguries.

Typical Tilehurst gambit: 'Are you going to the Motor Show this year?'

Guy Fawkes bonfires begin to take shape as early as the first week in October. If 5 November falls on a weekday, we have glimpses of them blazing – a chain of beacons from Paddington to Oxford. We spend an hour watching a zoetrope of burning guys, soaring rockets, falling stars, dancing children. A series of isolated moments in other people's enjoyment. Trapped in the train we can never see anything through, never participate. Our portion: spent fireworks and cold ashes.

Sunrise. Clear blue sky with white vapour trails. Some pencil-sharp. Others already blurring. Silver aeroplane at point of one, reeling off its magic line. Bright morning star.

The vapour trail: a person's past, growing vaguer as memory fades, till it vanishes altogether. Often people leave no visible trails at all – it depends on conditions.

The aeroplane equals Now – the split split split (*ad infinitum*) second present in an individual's life.

The surrounding blue stands for Time – past, present and future.

In front of the aeroplane – the pilot can gaze into it – lies the empty space of the future, empty, yet there waiting. As soon as the aeroplane enters it, and a portion of the vapour trail occupies it, the future ceases to exist and, passing rapidly through the present, becomes the past.

And what of the sun and the star? What of the observer

crawling on the rind of planet earth in an early morning train? All form parts of a model suspended in Eternity.

We must abandon Time's tempting games. Speculation about relativity, history, light years, distances of millions of miles, gets us nowhere. Time itself is a fast-fading vapour trail on the face of Eternity. Lucifer only *appears* steadfast and unchangeable – a treacherous example to follow. We have to learn to consider everything *sub specie aeternitatis*. Once we adopt this stance, a new life opens up. A life where commuting and mutability dwindle to insignificance, and belief in some kind of deity looms large. All change for regeneration.

ALTERNATIVE TITLE 8
The Waste Line.

For the train is full of shades. . .
    As the carriages flicker to and fro,
        To and fro:-
    O my Miller and my Durrell long ago!

COMMUTER'S CALENDAR 12
13 October: First Fierce Frost.

Paul Theroux in *The Great Railway Bazaar* says trains contain 'the essential paraphernalia of a nation's culture'. Indian trains prompted his observation, but it applies all too accurately to British ones. We, the commuters, represent the essential paraphernalia of British culture. In which case, God help British culture, and God help us.

And what can the many Indian and Pakistani employees of British Rail think of this state of affairs? Do they pine for the *te-rain* of Kim's India? A culture is no better than its trains – and their passengers.

TRAIN GAME 7
Assembling information about fellow-passengers. Ability to read quickly upside-down essential for this. Unscrupulousness and lack of principles also helpful. Names and addresses come from season tickets, correspondence, luggage labels, newsagents' scrawls on daily

papers. You gather most data from documents – place and nature of employment, salary, financial status, interests, and so on. You learn to identify office passes and recondite neck-ties. Occasionally you pick up snippets – or even nuggets – from overheard conversations.

Most people lay bare their lives remarkably freely; either from ignorance of the fact that to give strangers details about yourself is tantamount to giving nail-clippings and locks of hair to a black magician (you stand within his danger), or from confidence that they have nothing to hide. Only people like myself, blessed or cursed with prying-into habits and suspicious minds, do our obsessive best to give nothing away, while offering the greatest challenge to those, again like myself, who enjoy solving people as though they were crossword puzzles.

Still see from time to time women wearing obvious travelling outfits. They sit there enjoying their day out, oblivious of the less fashionably dressed riff-raff around them.

How often, when night has fallen and the train should have reached Oxford, have I gazed resignedly out of the window at Didcot to see the neon message: DRAGON HOTEL. How aptly named. Drag on. Drag on.

ANTI-KONTAKION 22

A curse on the train. Steed with voluntary Mazeppas strapped to its back. Trojan horse with involuntary invaders trapped in its belly. Non-stop stylus rendering parchment illegible. Decompression chamber making divers incapable. Cocoon in which souls may be woken. Wheel on which butterflies can be broken. Anathema sit.

DIALOGUE 6

Oxford Station. I am about to board the 0754. Supervisor accosts me:
'Sir, there's something you might like to know.'
'Yes?'
'On Monday week this train will leave at 0752 and stop at Radley.'

Life is a Platform – title of collection of poems by Peter Levi. His companion volume – *Death is a Pulpit*. Seems to me he

131

missed an opportunity. Death is a train, and we leave the platform at our peril.

Commuting essentially mental – in at least three senses. We *do* nothing. Galley-slaves at least had the physical act of rowing to take their minds off their predicament – no time to ask: *Que fais-je dans cette galère?* Mental, because not physical. Mental, because mad. Mental, because the train transports minds. The minds of those too bright and too stupid to stay at home. Bright enough to be courted by London employers. Stupid enough to fall for their blandishments. Minds attached to irrelevant bodies. Mindless minds. Minds which set out each Monday morning full of greenery and poetry, to arrive at Paddington all greyness and prose. Minds which carelessly bought their first season ticket while still alive with creative ideas, childhood memories, love, heroes, travels, hope, now make the nightly ritual pause beside Osney cemetery devoid of all these and crying for restful death. The train can erase a weekend in an hour, and in a few years a whole life.

MORE TRAVELLING TITLES
Fruitful and Responsible Love. The Culture of the Abdomen. A Scientific Approach to Hair Design. Continental Cross-Country in a Fokker Triplane Replica. The Organ. The Structure of Bifocal Distance. Unwanted Pregnancy – Accident or Illness? A Pocket Atlas of Arrhythmias.

In contrast to the accentless DEPOT at Reading, the beautiful diaeresis of CITROËN on a warehouse near Slough gladdens the bleary eyes of pedantic commuters.

Sapling-clad embankments by Pangbourne provoke yearning for lost hazel-thickets of Serbia.

OVERHEARD 11
Black girl (in search of God?): 'I've got to do a T. S. Eliot poem, but it's so uninspired.'

ALTERNATIVE TITLE 9
Travels with a Briefcase in the Home Counties.

OXFORD STATION 3
III

Bog, bog, bog, they all go into the bog,
Into the vacant tessellated bog;
La Société Nationale des Chemins de Fer Français,
The hack poet, the pornographer,
Dean Swift and Stella,
They all go into the bog.
Or I will put it another way,
No more or less satisfactory:

In the grimpen where fancy lights
The moving finger ever writes
And having writ moves on unseen
Leaving the more or less obscene,
Mene, mene, tekel upharsin,
This is the death of words.

Smuts on a small boy's face
Are the only remaining trace
In the locomotive's place;
Now that diesel rules the rail
Supplies of fumes will never fail
For our nostrils to inhale,
This is the death of steam.

Dear Notebook, I took you with me on holiday to Norfolk. There I started to leaf through you, and found I could not really understand why I had begun you. Hope you are not a wine that does not travel. Or a pebble that gleams in the train-aquarium, but out of water loses lustre.

TRACKSIDE INDUSTRY 9
Crane Packing Ltd. One imagines a team of budding Christos expertly swaddling jibs, booms, derricks, pulleys and graceful grues. Doubt if they get Christo's money. One day perhaps they will branch

out as he has done. Train packing, for instance, has possibilities.
What a challenge – to transform a commuter train into a work of art
by wrapping it in a huge shroud!

We take our pews for matins. Hymns and psalms as advertised in the timetable. Compulsory collection *en route*. Always a feeling of tension before morning service begins. I like to be seated in good time so as to collect my thoughts and watch other members of the congregation arrive.

OVERHEARD 12
'They both like to go to church on Sunday mornings, so it makes weekends very difficult.'

Growing realisation that *The Unquiet Grave*, with its hundred pages, is a *long* book. The writer of a Premeditated Notebook compiles his short entries slowly and leaves out much that might pad a more discursive work. The time and the omissions leave their mark.

COMMUTER'S CALENDAR 13
24 October: Daylight Diminishes. Damp Dripping Dew. Deciduous Decline, Decay and Death.

All evening trains should include at least one unlighted coach. One 30 October I found myself in one by accident. A kindly ticket-collector advised us: 'I shouldn't try to read in here. The battery's gone – you'll ruin your eyes.' Many fled and missed marvellous sunset and dusk. Nocturnal landscape one great Gromboolian Plain on which erratically roamed headlamps of forlorn Dongs.

OVERHEARD 13
Little girl to little boy: 'Our dog's stomach must be full of silver paper. Our cat opens the fridge and the dog eats the tops off the milk bottles.'

Infrequent pleasures enhanced, daily vicissitudes alleviated, by thought that all furnish grist for Notebook, my secret mistress.

LITERARY LANDMARK 8, PADDINGTON

When waiting on Paddington Station, I sometimes catch myself reflecting how soothing it might be to live one's whole life beneath the glass and metal canopy. One need never go outside – apart from the hotel and the usual buffets and bookstalls, Paddington also has a barber's, a heel bar, and a chemist's. I go on to think of writing a book on this theme. At this point my tired mind does a double-take and remembers with a jolt that the idea has already been brilliantly handled by John Wain in his brief, poignant The Smaller Sky.

Whether intentionally or not, Wain made the station itself the protagonist. With a minimum of straight description he works it so that, by the end of the book, the reader finds himself an inhabitant of the great terminus. Oddly, John Wain delivers the most explicit summing-up on Paddington through the mind of the least sympathetic character, a cynical go-getter. Perhaps he is thus indicating a certain glib superficiality in the statement:

He thought of the station ahead, its curious doubleness. At one level, the epitome of London: urban, crowded, for ever anchored by steel bands in its grimy setting. On another, weightless, floating, a place of transit to other places . . .

Paddington Station emerges from the story with credit. The villains prove once again to be that notorious pair: Getting and Spending.

Inside the *Stalag Zug* prisoners' attitudes to captivity vary. A few level-headed ones plan and effect escape. Many more dream of freedom without attempting to achieve it. Some retreat into a private trance. Others, captives void of noble rage, accept their lot, and devise ploys to relieve the tedium of long incarceration, such as scratching on the cell walls crude calendars, or messages to be found by hypothetical liberators who will certainly arrive too late. Commuting destroys red corpuscles, so we cannot use blood for ink. I laboriously scrawl these forbidden notes in lymph.

31 October: Foliage Falling Fast. Filemot. Freshness. Fog.

ANTI-KONTAKION 23
A curse on the train. Flight simulator. Fright stimulator. Wrecker of romances. Breaker of our fancies. Zip-fastener linking the disparate for a moment. Rude hastener sinking the desperate with its movements. Anathema sit.

The commuter is never more alone than when in a crowded train.

OVERHEARD 14
Middle-aged couple with First Class tickets (woman wearing two strings of pearls and *a gold necklace), finding no seats in First Class, took refuge with* hoi polloi *in Second. Man to wife: 'Never mind, dear. It will do us good.'*

The journey not the arrival matters – an outmoded concept, at least on English railways. Trend in trains towards an insulated capsule, an introverted container. Windows grow smaller and darker. Speeds increase. 'They' assume that people do not want to look out, and that, even if they did, nothing worth seeing would meet their eyes. Journeying no longer seen as an experience to savour, something embarked upon for its own sake, but as a boring necessity to be got over as quickly and as painlessly as possible.

This explains why Freya Stark and Patrick Leigh Fermor do not top the best-seller lists. They write the finest English prose going, but they use it to promulgate heretical ideas about the advantages of slow, difficult journeys with no certain destination. They digress, they dilate, they philosophise, they *think*. Subversive stuff! Counter to the spirit of the age. How fortunate that the reading public can discern the danger, and ostracizes these public enemies.

ALTERNATIVE TITLE 10
A Wonder Book of Travel.

On the fine bronze war memorial at Paddington a wreath with the message: In Remembrance Area Manager And Staff Paddington. Especially as train services at the time were chaotic, I read this as evidence that the Area Manager and Staff had departed, leaving Paddington in a state of anarchy. This struck me as amusing, but fellow-commuters, with whom I tried to share the joke, were shocked. They could not see the difference between disrespect for the glorious dead, and gentle mockery of plastic laurel leaves, paper poppies and a lack of punctuation. I did not press the point, but sat reflecting that men had died in two world wars that we might commute in safety. When will 'They' erect a monument to the Unknown Commuter? He could stand between the brooding Brunel and the monstrous effigy of Paddington Bear.

MYSTERY 3 (continued)

Curious discovery that first six words of carefully executed graffito, FAR AWAY IS CLOSE AT HAND IN IMAGES OF ELSEWHERE, *form the first line of a poem by Robert Graves entitled* Song of Contrariety. *Nowhere in the rather opaque poem do the last four words appear. The information only compounds the mystery.*

Stop Press: On 18 June 1981 at 0910 we saw man with sledge-hammer beginning to demolish wall bearing graffito. By 1805 all that remained was WHERE. Those nine and a half words had clearly not gone down without a struggle.

Have been catching various trains lately, and hardly sitting in the same place two days running. This perplexes the regulars who, if they do glimpse me, say things like: 'We heard you'd been chopping and changing', 'Someone said they'd seen you', 'Why do you do it?' It amuses me to play the elusive Scholar Commuter, to fly feverish contact with my fellows, to avoid the infection of their mental strife, to ruffle their routine and boost my own ego. But who am I trying to kid? No nook or cranny of the train remains untainted by:

> This strange disease of modern life,
> With its sick hurry, its divided aims,
> Its head o'ertaxed, its palsied hearts . . .

(Arnold himself used to commute and died running for a tram.) Only away from the train can physical, mental and spiritual health be found. I must decamp and take my corded bales elsewhere before the merchandise perishes and becomes unsaleable.

A question to ponder: 'Is this train right for Oxford?'

Recommendation from R.: 'Try travelling without a brief-case. Wear old clothes. Take your tie off. You'll feel as if you're on holiday. Try it.' Yes, the tourist approach. Much to be said for it. Better to be open, naïve, excited, curious, gawping, communicative, smiling, than uptight, buttoned up, world-weary, knowing, silent, frowning. But better far to be all these things off the train.

OVERHEARD 15

'And she gave me a koala bear, a kangaroo and a duck-billed platypus.'

A couple kissing at a factory door.

Man accosting stranger on train: 'I say, isn't that oilseed rape?' (Pointing at passing crop.) Stranger utterly non-plussed.

On Friday nights when the hordes have gone home, when 1900 becomes 7 p.m., out ventures the British Rail Western Region Staff Military Band to exploit the superb acoustics of The Lawn. Lumps rise in throats, eyes blur, as men (predominantly) and women of all ages, with beer at their feet, produce their stirring, brazen stuff. Who are they? Booking clerks? Guards? Engine-drivers? Porters? Cleaners? I know not. But their music unites them, transforms them, welds them continuously into an entity which transcends BR and ASLEF and the NUR and commuting, which makes nonsense of everything but this, where the whole consort momentarily dances together on a pin's head.

HEADLINE 7
Willey's Last Stand.

If you put a British Rail plastic or cardboard cup to your ear you can hear the train.

> God helpe the man so wrapt in Errours endlesse traine!
> (Spenser: *The Faerie Queene*)

Do I repeat myself? Very well then I repeat myself. An aged Theban once handed me his notebook and asked me to write down my name and address. I did so. He turned over some pages and made me repeat the procedure. And again. And again. But why? 'Because,' he explained, 'the more times your name and address are written in my notebook, the easier it will be for me to find them when I want them.' He sat in a courtyard among great whitewashed slabs of Cadmean masonry. Perhaps a reincarnation of Tiresias himself.

From the *New Review*: 'Why are tired commuters in trains more willing to read book reviews than books?' What an odd idea! In my experience totally untrue. You seldom see a commuter reading *The Times Literary Supplement*, let alone the *New Review*. All that tired commuters ask are undemanding books that will afford them an hour's escape without provoking worrying thoughts about escaping for good.

Commuting = purgatory. Yes. Undeniable. But purgatory, thank God, not a final state, only a preparation for heaven. So maybe I should count myself blessed to have this opportunity of working my passage to paradise. Who knows how many indulgences I may already have earned?

Hazards of commuting: A. put his hand into his pocket and brought it out bleeding. 'I cut it on my season ticket,' he explained.

Commuting: a drug beneficial in small amounts, but fatal in overdose.

A coprophilous small boy, I was fascinated one day, as we walked along the sleepers, when a friend pointed out to me human excreta in various stages of decomposition from fresh and steaming, when a train had just passed, to shrivelled and dry. A major revelation. It had never occurred to me before that, when you flushed the lavatory on the train, the stuff went straight out on to the track. Too simple.

No wonder 'They' tried to discourage trespassers. 'They' were not worried about people being maimed or decapitated. 'They' did not want it generally known that the permanent way is an open sewer, and that trains are great defecating freaks which lack the wit to soil anything but the same narrow strip day in day out.

All that we commuters need to do to leave the stercoraceous zone behind is step a foot or two to either side of the metals. So easy. Yet, conditioned to believe ourselves hopelessly bogged down, we continue to travel to and fro over our own excrement. In transit. In trainshit. Dung and death.

Travelled one morning on 0712 opposite a man known for his television appearances. He snoozed. Ticket-collector woke him up very gently, saying: 'Sorry to disturb you, sir.' Unprecedented.

COMMUTER'S CALENDAR 15
November: Numbing Nights. No Note-making. Narcosis. Near Nadir Now.

When period arrives during which we have to journey both ways in darkness, we become doubly dungeoned – by the train and by the night enclosing the train. In summer we look outwards. In winter, of necessity, we look inwards – and make disturbing discoveries.

ALTERNATIVE TITLE 11
Metaphors.

The train: a halloween pumpkin-shell. Commuters: guttering candles giving the death-mask a mocking semblance of life.

Don't tell anyone, but I like sitting still doing nothing. At home and at work one gets reproached for this. On the train (as long as one cultivates an air of stoical resignation to suffering) one can get away with it. Over duck-decoy funnel entrance to Paddington a coat of arms carries the motto: *Domine dirige nos virtute et industria.* My retort to such pomposity: *Dulce est desipere in loco.*

ANTI-KONTAKION 24
A curse on the train. Treadmill. Tumbril. Penance. Durance. Inducer of neurosis. Producer of narcosis. Stooge of devils. Scourge of revels. Loather of all laughter. Lover of disaster. Anathema sit.

Train exceedingly like cave in Plato's *Republic*. Under a form of constraint, we believe what we experience to be reality. No way of knowing all sights shadows, all sounds echoes. No desire to escape because glimpses of true light only dazzle and confuse us. Happy with our systems of honours and commendations.

Somehow, even though unwilling, we have to be 'brought up to the light, just as certain heroes are said to have ascended from Hades to the gods above', to start 'the true ascent which leads towards being'. Corollary – that, having managed to break out and discover real life, we have a duty to return to the world of fettered troglodytes – doesn't bear thinking about.

Serendipitous discovery – in the Twenties some bright sparks founded the Oxford Railway Club, in order to travel on trains in style, declaiming verses and being generally aesthetic. In 1963 the survivors hired a Pullman coach from Oxford Station for a reunion, and who should be among them but old *miglior fabbro* Palinurus himself. An auspicious coincidence. Not much style to the London Nod these days.

COMMUTER'S CALENDAR 16
8 December: Daylight Decreasing. Darkness Denser. Disheartening Drag. Disease Decimates. Deep Doubts. Dangerous Deathwish.

It's a battlefield, the landscape we pass through. Specifically, a Paul Nash battlefield where man's absence expresses his presence in the wings, or in the train. Your name could be here. Each day we entrain for the front. The rumble of the guns grows louder as we approach London. We go to gain a little patch of ground that hath in it no profit but the name. The war perpetuates itself in our minds. We long for the Blighty one that will ensure an honourable discharge, not realising that the empty fields, woods, streets, have been won, have been liberated long since, and lie there waiting to be possessed. Tanks rust. Blasted stumps sprout. Flooded shell-craters reflect a blue sky empty of bombers. Robins nest in the mouths of guns. Foxes and badgers inhabit the trenches. If we would only claim it, no man's land belongs to us.

Sometimes a goods train passes, wheels dripping sparks, like horse splashing through sunlit water.

HEADLINE 8
Girl Would Not Get Up In Morning.

Most of us carry briefcases of orthodox design. Some civil servants have cryptic notices on theirs instructing the finder to return same to 'the address on the other side of this label'. They hope everyone will think they work for MI5. They need the cover to hide the humdrum nature of their jobs. Some people have hold-alls bursting with junk and newspapers. Lawyers tote laundry-bags containing soiled collars. But only A., among those known to me, has achieved real originality. He uses a battered cardboard suitcase covered in paper printed with a crocodile-skin pattern. On one side a sticker asks: Have You Thanked A Green Tree Today? Yet even he upstaged by those who manage with no burden at all.

Shunters: the lock-keepers of the railway, with their long poles and placid, unhurrying, knowledgeable air.

At night from my house can see Oxford Station romantically glimmering about two miles away, like every meretricious allurement that has ever enticed a man from home and family – fool's gold, will-o'-the-wisp, a mirage of Midas, the philosopher's stone, Jack-o'-lantern, corposant, St Elmo's fire, *fata Morgana*. An *ignis fatuus* which never fails to attract me. The rainbow's end. A delusive flame towards which, mothlike, I struggle again and again.

DIALOGUE 7

Self to American newcomer: 'What do you think of commuting so far?'
Transatlantic neophyte: 'I guess I've been sold a load of goods.'

The train = Moby Dick, the Great White Whale himself:

Yet calm, enticing calm, oh, whale! thou glidest on, to all who for the first time eye thee, no matter how many in that same way thou may'st have bejuggled and destroyed before.

Should like people to call me Ishmael. Should like to feel I have a chance of making a coffin my lifebuoy. But fear I have too much of Captain Ahab in me. The train obsesses me more and more:

He tasks me; he heaps me; I see in him outrageous strength, with an inscrutable malice sinewing it. That inscrutable thing is what I chiefly hate . . .

Ahab's sunset speech clinches the parallel with another of those uncanny, clairvoyant remarks:

The path to my fixed purpose is laid with iron rails, whereon my soul is grooved to run.

Ahab declared himself to be 'madness maddened'. Hope my own lunacy is of a healthier sort. I aim to rescue my shipmates and myself from the *stultifera navis*, before the Whale gets us, not to drown and take them all with me. Let Ahab stand as a warning, not a model.

To us waiting on Didcot Station, approaching train announces itself by transmitting along the rails the twittering sound of pebbles thrown across a frozen lake, or of suppliant souls of the unburied dead.

On a seat in 0712 at Oxford one morning, fresh bird-droppings.

Oxford supervisor on possible improvements in rolling-stock: 'We've been promised a full set for next year.' ('Full set' suggests to me naval beard and sidewhiskers, but not in dictionary as a phrase.)

ALTERNATIVE TITLE 12
Viewfoils.

Ticket-collector explained to disoriented passenger: 'The front of the train is where the engine is.' All right, but at the time the train had not left Paddington. When a train full of passengers comes in to the terminus, clearly the engine is in front towing the train. But when empty trains arrive from the carriage sidings pulled by engines, what then? At what point does the back become the front? High Speed Trains (so-called) complicate matters further by always having a working locomotive at each end. How do worms decide?

COMMUTER'S CALENDAR 17
16 December: Freezing Fog First. Fireball Phoebus Follows. Feathery Fronds. Fantastic Faery Farms, Fields, Factories, Filigree

Fringed Fences. Frost-Freaked Furrows. Flocks of Foraging Field-fares. Folk Fare Forward in Fusty Frowst.

Caught a mid-morning train as feeling fragile after illness. Realisation that such trains also have their regulars – has-beens who feel fragile all the time. Typical of their kind: middle-aged military men pretending (to themselves as well as to others) to be so grand, so important that they do not need to be in the office before midday. Working out their pensionable years, dreeing their weird, from a misguided sense of honour. Too proud to give up, to give in before retirement releases them. That convalescent morning I felt dangerously akin to such veterans.

> So better with the happy
> Discover than with the wise
> Who teach the sad valour
> Of endurance through the seasons.
>   (Lawrence Durrell)

(Oxford) DIALOGUE 8
'Is anyone actually *sitting here?'*
'Well, I gather *someone is.'*

Discovery (unoriginal, but every writer has to make it for himself) of how each entry in Notebook – not to mention each sentence, each word – shifts, alters, modifies all that has gone before. Entries influence each other, interreact. Cannot find the right metaphor. A possible approximation: once I witnessed a serious crime and glimpsed the perpetrator. Ever since, I have been struggling to build up an indentikit picture of the man. Each added feature puts the others into a new perspective. One day, perhaps, I shall add one more wart or wrinkle, and everything will click into place. Meanwhile I continue to help with inquiries.

Extraordinary nature of such conversation as does take place on the train. Nowhere else (except mental hospitals) do people suddenly switch off animated talk to read or sleep. Nowhere else do people accept such behaviour. In this respect our journeys resemble nightmare of an endless, unsuccessful dinner party.

ALTERNATIVE TITLE 13
Down and Out in between Oxford and Paddington.

Everything affects us. Everything impinges. 'Will three wise men, travelling to Bethlehem, please call at King Herod's office on the main concourse.' 'The 1914 has been cancelled owing to an incident at Sarajevo.' 'Will an ayatollah go to the Teheran end of Platform 15.' Each man's death diminishes us.

That face in the street we vaguely recognise. It always turns out that we saw it in one of two settings of similar remoteness and unreality – television or the train.

COMMUTER'S CALENDAR 18
31 December: Unreal Unkind Unnatural Unseason.

Democracy in action at Oxford one evening:

① A well-known, noble, slightly fuddled lord. ② A conscientious ticket-inspector. ③ Beyond the gate, a uniformed chauffeur with limousine, waiting for ①. ② remained adamant that ① could not pass to ③ until he had found his ticket. Did not wait to see the resolution, but by the following morning the tableau had gone.

Occasionally, passing through Paddington in the middle of the day, I have surprised the loudspeakers broadcasting musak, as farmers do in milking-sheds to increase yield.

'They' would not dare inflict it on commuters. Anyway, 'They' do not need to.

Now, children, here are some auxiliary verbs – another example of the richness of the English language: may, can, will, must, might, could. See how many of them you can fit into this sentence: We regret any inconvenience this ——————— cause. What else might fill the blank?

A February morning. We whizz past Tilehurst where hordes on riparian platform await their stopping train. Down-stream a huge red fireball suffuses the sky with its colour, the water with its reflection. A staggering sunrise which the Tilehurstians have only to turn their heads to see. Instead, they all gaze morosely at the tracks as if contemplating mass suicide.

ANTI-KONTAKION 25
A curse on the train. Plato's cave. Dante's inferno. Donne's gallows-cart. Emily Dickinson's chariot. Melville's whale. Kavafy's city. Kafka's castle. Kipling's te-rain. Palinurus's unquiet grave. Greene's battlefield. Sartre's huis clos. Orwell's room 101. Empson's poison. Anathema sit.

A. has dubbed Didcot commuters 'the Didicoits'.

TRACKSIDE INDUSTRY 10
Emanuel, Sigmund, Suterwalla, Wonka, Pasold. Names redolent of the proud excitement of making good in a foreign land, of sticking your monicker up on a big board read by thousands every day.

Commuters are by definition mad. Mad with the icy, humourless, rational, sane madness of a Hitler. The train our lunatic asylum in which 'They' allow us a lot of freedom because 'They' know 'They' can trust us not to turn violent. D.C.T. or Diesel Convulsive Therapy works wonders. When a gloriously, splendidly mad original, such as a London tramp or an Oxford don, strays on to our train, we cringe in fear and horror.

Orate pro nobis: William Huskisson, Alastair Grahame, Henry Treece.

COMMUTER'S CALENDAR 19
8 February: Mild. Misty. Moorhens Madly Mating in Middle of Mere.

The train: a wilderness, a Thebaïd. Commuters: a colony of hermits. As time goes by we merge more and more into our arid surroundings. Our existence a travesty of the genuine ascetic way. We never see visions, only hallucinations. We hear mocking voices, never the true word. The only way we can derive any benefit from these lost years is by struggling through the desert back into the world. Then both our new life and the old *via negativa* will assume their proper perspective.

I saw eternity the other night – a clock at Paddington with no face, only an incandescent white neon ring, searing its image on the retina. If exhibited at the ICA, critics would call it at worse clever, at best genius.

Having written the previous note, thought I would check the Henry Vaughan quotation. Have a good repertoire of titles and first lines, but seldom remember what follows. Stunned to find this:

The World

> I saw Eternity the other night
> Like a great *Ring* of pure and endless light,
>   All calm, as it was bright,
> And round beneath it, Time in hours, days, years
>   Driven by the spheres
> Like a vast shadow mov'd, in which the world
>   And all her train were hurl'd . . .

And all her train! So it continues. I recommend any commuter to read the whole, incredibly apt poem, as I have now just done. (He even uses the word 'madness'.)

Must have read it before, but had totally forgotten all but that first line which the faceless clock called to mind.

Vaughan, of course, had never heard of electric clocks with lights inside, or of railway trains and commuters. But, like Gray, quoted earlier, he *knew*. Poets *know*. And I take the fact that I keep stumbling on these germane quotations as a token of the existence of the means of grace and the hope of glory.

A lovely sight when ticket-inspector throws back compartment door and eight pieces of cardboard flash as one. You would have to be incredibly quick on draw to claim title of 'the fastest season ticket in the Western Region'.

Dressed in the clothes of victims or of suspects (no significant distinction), day after day we revisit the scene, re-enact the crime. Day after day we miss the clues.

Notebook like birds' nest soup – a delicacy made from unpleasant ingredients.

Poets walk into the fields to spend their hour. Commuters step into the train to squander theirs.

HEADLINE 9
Man Fought Woman In Self Defence.

Read in the *New Review* the other day an article by Jonathan Cook about the *Prison Notebooks* and *Letters from Prison* of Antonio Gramsci. Cook speaks of Gramsci's writings showing him 'struggling to maintain a grasp on the outside world'. I do not, I repeat, take myself too seriously. Notebook not a *De Profundis*, but a *De Vadis*. All the same, commuters do have more in common with the Bunyan-Wilde-Pound-Gramsci axis than we should like to think. We have minds which, had it not been for our commuting, could have blossomed in all sorts of directions. Those minds, paradoxically, have led to our incarceration. We find ourselves not so much political as socio-economical prisoners. As Mussolini demanded in Gramsci's case, so the chilling order has gone out for each one of us: 'We must prevent this brain from functioning for twenty years.' By writing we can at least make a show of resistance. We cannot hope to preserve our faculties intact, but we may slow up the process of mental attrition. Reaching readers a secondary consideration.

Jonathan Cook writes: 'Imprisonment removed Gramsci from the immediate contexts of conflict and argument that he needed to validate his own thought.' If one may great things to small compare, the same fate befalls commuters. Our thoughts become invalidated. We become invalid. Ours (dare I suggest) possibly an even more pernicious position because of our illusion of freedom. The prisoner in gaol cannot deceive himself. He knows he is floundering in the deeps, and he can cry out or not, depending on his articulacy, will-power and self-discipline. Most of us do not even feel the water lapping round our feet, while only a handful sense the dangerous undertow. Not waving but drowning. The prisoner is whelmed in deeper gulfs than we who, like Palinurus, perish in the shallows. All can derive solace from the motto of the Royal Humane Society: *Lateat scintillula forsan.* That tiny spark may yet save us.

ALTERNATIVE TITLE 14
The Story of my Death.

It took me two and a half years to solve the DORMAR-RAMROD conundrum. Over three to spot the link between Didcot power station and Wittenham Clumps. Over five to experience the apocalypse of the faceless clock and Vaughan's Eternity. What further epiphanies can I look forward to? Freya Stark, quoting Heracleitus: 'If you do not expect the unexpected you will not find it; for it is hard to be sought out and difficult.' Yes, but such rare revelations scarcely justify mortgaging one's soul. Off the train the unexpected manifests itself daily. Alexander Pope prophetically describes the price of remaining on the train:

> On all the line a sudden vengeance waits,
> And frequent hearses shall besiege your gates:
> There passengers shall stand . . .

We have been warned.

Sometimes see my former headmaster, well over 65, on train. He proudly draws attention to his concessionary ticket franked with the word CHILD. While an Oxford ticket-seller told me one day: 'Students get half price, and elderly people like yourself suffer.' One more example of how the train turns the world inside-out. Old men become as little children; young men grow prematurely old; and students, lured by smiles, soap and cheap railway tickets, start unsuspectingly on the downward track.

OVERHEARD 16

Fusspot at Oxford inquiring whether guard has turned heating on (on a mild morning too): 'Has he attended to the mechanism at the back of the carriage?'

Unexpected food for commuting thought – or what passes for thought with us – in catalogue of Millet exhibition:

He was convinced that man is condemned forever to bear his burdens, hence he made the peasant into a victim of unyielding fate that kept him in the unchanging cycle of work and exhausted repose, the cycle that had been his lot since ancient times.

But Millet's message became twisted after his death:

The peasant could actually personify that vital principle of the middle class: the morality of labour. [He] became the embodiment of the very work ethic that underlay bourgeois aspirations of the nineteenth century. To work hard and to carve out a place in society by individual effort is the very credo of the many morality books which the middle class thrived upon.

The writer has not taken his argument far enough. A revolution has occurred. Not a French Revolution, but the kind that involves things going round, as train wheels go round. As they go round they come back to where they started. The middle-class commuter has become the peasant his nineteenth century forerunners admired. No question for him of 'carving out a place in society' as he struggles to survive 'in the unchanging cycle of work and exhausted repose'. No time or energy left to read morality books (whatever they were) or meditate upon the work ethic.

Our wives stay at home and grow vegetables while we, totally swinked, plough interminably up and down the shining sillions of the railway, without making the slightest impression. We glean where wheat never grew. Unquestioning victims. Heaven help the twenty-first century if it tries to set us up as models to be emulated. The man with the hoe and the man with the season ticket are one.

COMMUTER'S CALENDAR 20
5 March: Vapour Veils. Vague Vegetation. Vanishing Views. Variable Visibility.

Old couple who boarded train at Oxford worried about alighting at Reading. 'This isn't the door we came in by, dear, you know.' In end like trapped sparrows they fluttered whole length of coach so as to leave by door of their original entry. Some Greeks believe that, when visiting a house for first time, you court disaster if you exit through any other door than the one you entered by. Maybe this elderly pair motivated by similar superstition.

Wisdom of Nikos Kazantzakis in *Christ Recrucified*, describing train as: 'the machine of the devil, brought by the Franks, curse them!'

ANTI-KONTAKION 26
A curse on the train. Barmecide. Bromide. Terminator of love. Annihilator of life. Restriction of hope. Constriction of scope. Ordeal without relief. Ritual without belief. Anathema sit.

On some trucks the word Dewsnap. A place? A codename? Prestwin another. First has delightful ambiguity of cowslip. Second suggests vats of intoxicating must. No need to know their significance. Negative capability the order of the day. Doubt wisely. Cannot see mail-vans marked Foss Island Train without remembering Edward Lear's cat, or the instruction Return To Tintern Quarry without thinking of Wordsworth's return to the steep and lofty cliffs. Romance brings up goods trains in an esoteric world where commuter destinations like Oxford and Paddington take second place to powerful cult centres such as Didcot and Old Oak Common, Western Region's Stonehenge and Dodona.

The military jargon word 'detrain' much more aptly applied to the process a commuter – if he is to survive – must undergo on quitting train for good. As agents need debriefing, so we need detraining.

This Buffet Will Be Open For The Service Of Food And Drink At . . . Compare and contrast: This Church Will Be Open For The Service Of Holy Communion At . . .

Paradoxically, the train seldom encounters resistance at Maidenhead. Reading presents the problems, plays hard to get. Reading seldom wants it. Most mornings no amount of cajoling will switch her signals to 'come' or lubricate her frigid points. Either the train has to force its way slowly and painfully through, stopping and starting, even, occasionally, retreating a little to gain more; or it must violently rape. O the thrill of raping Reading! The rare thrill when a non-stop train decides to override her coyness, girds its pistons, charges, and penetrates, brooking no delaying tactics. Ungallant. Cruel. But no more than she deserves – the fickle bitch!

TRAIN GAME 8
Pub-spotting. Those with good eyesight can excel at this game, spying half-hidden inn-signs down unlikely back streets. But be warned! It is an exercise in extreme masochism.

Wheels over points at speed embroider a Gene Krupa solo – loose-wristed, relaxed, irresistible.

ALTERNATIVE TITLE 15
The Leaden Notebook.

Commuting teaches tolerance. Because, obviously, the more you complain about smokers, fresh-air fanatics etc., the more you hasten death from apoplexy. But also because tomorrow you may need the friendship of the tiresome sniffer sitting opposite you today.

LITERARY LANDMARK 9, SUMMING-UP

Seven or eight landmarks spread over sixty miles – not bad going. Could have increased the number by adding Windsor Castle (Pope, Ainsworth etc.) and Taplow (Walter De La Mare once lived there). Doubtless, too, I have missed other opportunities through nescience. (Dear Tiresias, You appear to have overlooked the 24-book poem on chiropody by a mid-nineteenth-century vicar of Elthorne, the Reverend Seymour Clipcorn Foot . . .)

What strikes me, looking back on the list, is a suggestion that topographical writing can secure a degree of immortality even for writers not of the highest calibre. This encourages me. I have a modest aspiration to make a sixty-mile stretch of British Rail (W) my own. To possess it and be possessed by it in order to secure release from its continuously welded fetters.

Sir John Betjeman may never have set himself a similar aim, but, willy-nilly, he has become the poet of the old G.W.R. As I trundle to and fro seeking remission and absolution, I think of and comprehend his stanza:

> *The old Great Western Railway shakes,*
> *The old Great Western Railway spins,*
> *The old Great Western Railway makes*
> *Me very sorry for my sins.*

We travel eastwards in the morning, westwards in the evening. A grey tide governed by no natural laws. We made only two mistakes. The first: setting out. The second: returning. Archetypal fortune-seekers travel onwards for at least a year and a day, often for longer, before coming home successful. Night after night we abort our quest. Instead of a crock of gold, all we have to show is a computerised payslip. Instead of a grail, a tupperware sandwich-box.

COMMUTER'S CALENDAR 21

12 March: Blackthorn Blossom Beginning.

Announcers have misleading habit of referring to departing

trains by their destinations. They speak of 'the 1800 to Worcester' and 'the 1803 to Oxford', for instance, without mentioning that the former will take you non-stop to Oxford in under an hour, while the latter, calling at many stations, takes over an hour and a half.

Equally confusing is their custom of distinguishing incoming trains by their time and station of origin. If you go to Paddington to meet a friend from Plymouth arriving at 1640, and you hear an announcement concerning the 1140 from Penzance, you need all your wits about you to realise that this means your friend's train.

Once again the hospital analogy applies. 'They' in 'Their' wisdom believe a patient should not be told too much. If he or she happens to know enough Greek to interpret the arcane jargon, that is his or her good or bad luck.

I travelled lonely in the crowd, that daily goes by British Rail, when all at once I glimpsed, beside the tracks at Royal Oak, a solitary daffodil. It hung its head forlornly, struggling for survival among clinkers and ballast. A prose-writer could not but be sad. No time to gaze and gaze. The train shot past. If I hadn't jotted it down in Notebook, I would have forgotten it before Paddington. I sometimes wish I had.

DIALOGUE 9
Suave, assured, wizard-prang chap: 'We've met before. Were you not in the RAF?'
Self: 'Certainly not!'

John Wain says that when he travels he becomes 'more of a commercial traveller than a writer'. Says he has been known to work on poems on the train, but never novels. He suggested Rider Haggard wrote *King Solomon's Mines* on trains, but cannot find hard evidence for this. Kenneth Grahame's claim to the title of commuter-writer also appears weak. Somebody else advanced John Buchan as a possible candidate. Trouble is commuters have no time for thorough research. So far, though, Trollope remains the only genuine commuter-writer I have discovered. Did, however, catch John Le Carré, in a television interview, saying that he wrote his first book while commuting from Great Missenden.

Graham Greene, Paul Theroux and David Nobbs (to name but three) have all written about commuting. This does not make them – or me – commuter-writers. Besides which, they have not understood commuting. They have not understood that, for a commuter, commuting is not incidental, but central. Most commuters themselves do not realise this – there lies the petty tragedy. For anyone who spends more than two hours a day travelling to and from work, home and office become the incidentals. The train shapes, makes, controls and breaks him. Train-life takes over from real life.

> In the woods of the North there are insects which prey
> On the brain of the elk till his very last sigh.
> (Thomas Moore)

The train preys on the mind of the commuter, who goes about his daily business quite unaware of the deadly parasite inside his cerebrum. Graham Greene has his latest anti-hero commute from Berkhamstead to MI6. He explores this man's character in terms of his past as a spy and as a family man. He and everyone else miss the point. In any thriller or whodunnit about commuters there is only one villain – the train dunnit.

Another illustration of the difficulty of being original. Since I advocated that every coach should carry a Government Health Warning, I have noticed several carriages marked in small letters: Warning Pressurized System. Have also spotted waiting inconspicuously in sidings a ready made-up train labelled Breakdown Unit.

OVERHEARD 17

Harassed middle-aged commuter accosting younger, less harassed ditto: 'Excuse me, are you the chap with whom I broke off a conversation in my office just now?'
'No.'
'Are you in the Civil Service?'

'No.'
'So sorry, my mistake.'

Man with perfect white hair, pinstripe suit – all the accoutrements – idealised businessman from an advertisement – reads, behind raised lid of his expensive black leather attaché case, like a naughty schoolboy, *Private Eye*. His stern expression never changes. Can only think he is an aristocratic backwoodsman who dreams of achieving fame and fortune through a libel suit.

HEADLINE 10
Bank To Issue Statement On Thames Depositors.

†Train, *sb.*[2] late ME. [a. OF. *traïne* guile f. OF. *traïr* (F. *trahir*) to betray.] 1. Treachery, guile, deceit, trickery – 1600. b. With *a* and *pl.* A trick, stratagem, artifice, wile – 1767. 2. A trap or snare for catching wild animals. (In phr. *to lay a t.*, assoc. with or merged in senses of TRAIN *sb.*[1]) – 1697. 3. A lure, bait, decoy –1602.

1. b. *Mach*, iv. iii. 118. 2. Caught in the T. which thou thyself hast laid DRYDEN.

A charm against commuting
THE VICIOUS CIRCLE

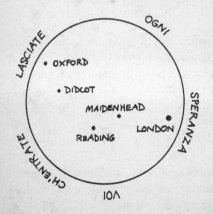

Salvation-aims:
(1) a home anywhere outside this vicious circle

(2) a job within cycling distance of home
(3) no railway station within ten miles
(4) the opportunity to visit Greece at least once a year.

ALTERNATIVE TITLE 16
Autopsy of a Commuter.

Coming out of London, on the right hand side we see nothing that could be called a field until the Flexello Castors sports ground at Taplow. On the left, here and there, a few green patches remain. At Southall half a dozen improbable donkeys await the Second Coming with the resignation of Eeyore. Near West Drayton a few cattle half-heartedly crop mangy grass. The scene somehow looks wrong. Too many broken bricks litter the meadow. The animals change too often. Shades of the abattoir. Only after Maidenhead does the true country begin.

Why the tendency towards smaller, tinted windows which do not open; towards air-conditioning; towards fast trains which only stop at one or two stations? The answer lies in history – 1917, Lenin and company passing through Germany in a macabre sealed train. The Germans gave permission for Lenin to travel from Switzerland in this manner because they hoped he might 'spread disaffection among the Russian soldiery'. (Should like to know how they sealed the train.)

Have never understood the niceties of war. You may bomb, shoot, maim, kill, but you must try not to destroy historic buildings or torture prisoners. If one of the enemy spies for you and is caught, he's a hero. If one of your side spies for the enemy and is caught, he's a traitor. (One day, incidentally, I hope to understand what Richard Nixon did wrong.) If a revolutionary wishes to travel through your country, he may – but only, according to the rules, in a sealed train. Crazy, as commuting is crazy. Commuting: another adult game, like war and politics, which everybody takes extremely seriously.

Obviously 'They' have concluded a secret agreement with the administrators of the land we journey through. All the time 'They' are working on ways of sealing our trains more securely. 'Their' deviousness knows no limits. We think we have rumbled 'Their' ploy. We feel flattered that 'They' should consider us budding Bolsheviks who might spread disaffection – without pausing to wonder where we might spread it. Fond fools! In this parable we represent the Russian soldiery. 'They' seal our trains to prevent us being tampered with by subversive forces which lie in ambush along the track. A latter-day Lenin lurks in the landscape, trying to get his message through to us: that the war has no point, that we are being exploited, that we should lay down our arms and return to our homes.

The Germans lived to regret giving Lenin a *laissez-passer* in 1917. If I have my way, 'They' will live to regret 'Their' attempt to isolate us and immunise us against real life. 'Their' enemy already has his agents in place, sleepers waiting for the right moment. 'They' can seal the train more effectively still. 'They' can lock the doors. 'They' can use troops. All to no avail, because the moles are already at work on the inside. All 'Their' security measures come too late. Meanwhile, our slogan once again: Commuters of the world unite! You have nothing to lose but your trains!

TRACKSIDE INDUSTRY 11
Mine Safety Appliances Ltd. Irresistible picture of chastity belts or clumsy Boswellian contraceptives. 'Come, Madam, let me roger you, but tarry while I don mine safety appliance.'

Early April in Goring Gap: green hedges with a dusting of blossom; green fields with a dusting of chalk; everything with a dusting of snow.

Train inimical to all human intercourse. In particular it nullifies significance and sanctity of physical contact. Thigh pressed to thigh, knee to knee, pretty girl's sleepy head on strange man's shoulder – all mean nothing except to a dedicated frotteur.

Those empty formulae again: 'We apologise for the inconvenience/any inconvenience/the considerable inconvenience this has caused/is causing/will/may/must cause etc.' Carefully graded like hospital bulletins – good, fair, satisfactory, serious, grave, critical – where 'satisfactory', for instance, means 'very ill' in ordinary language. Cf. too, diplomatic communiqués where 'frank and meaningful discussions' signify 'bitter disagreements' and 'cordial' is synonymous with 'cold'. Scales of obfuscation.

OVERHEARD 18
Man discussing stocks and shares: 'What I'm getting at is that it is a bona fide fiasco.'

ANTI-KONTAKION 27
A curse on the train. Parody of paradise. Paradigm of paradox. Train-washer. Brain-squasher. Paralyser. Vaporizer. Rusher of those who ought not to be hurried. Crusher of those who are tired and worried. Anathema sit.

What distinguishes commuter from ordinary traveller? Train beneficial for latter, deleterious to former. Commuter takes train daily to get nowhere. Traveller catches train occasionally to go somewhere. One man's ordeal. Another man's adventure. For further distinctions see Notebook *passim*. In Notebook I am trying to bridge great gulf fixed between the two, by exploiting the benefits – opportunity of leisure to observe everything inside and outside train; the hour's release from responsibility and inhibition that encourages free association, hatches thoughts – in order to neutralise disadvantages.

HEADLINE 11
London Bridge Quote Freeze.

Fewer branch-lines and junctions than there used to be. Fewer options, fewer connections.

ALTERNATIVE TITLE 17
Christianity and the Art of Locomotive Defiance.

In *The Marriage of Heaven and Hell*, as well as in some of his other jottings – e.g. his *Memorable Fancies and Proverbs of Hell* (a fool sees not the same train a wise man sees) – William Blake shows leanings towards the Premeditated Notebook. He adds the ingredient of his own illustrations. The P.N. a good medium for exploring such difficult territory as the soul of man. The terse, separate yet connected statements of the P.N. may happen upon truths obscured by continuous, flowing argument.

> On a huge hill,
> Cragged, and steep, Truth stands, and hee that will
> Reach her, about must, and about must goe;
> And what the hills suddennes resists, winne so.
>   (John Donne)

COMMUTER'S CALENDAR 22
22 March: Summer time So Sunset Seen from Six-fifteen.

What about Samuel Butler? His *Notebooks* were published posthumously, but he lavished so much care on them that he has a claim to be considered as a P.N. writer. He used to make his initial notes on scraps of paper. Later he would polish these and put them in the Notebook proper. Later still he would go through his Notebooks weeding out items he thought superfluous, and touching up still further what remained. He had no over all theme, but simply dealt with whatever was occupying his mind at the moment. Naturally certain obsessions recur. Paradoxically, then, Samuel Butler managed to turn the one kind of notebook – the writer's random ragbag – into the other, the P.N. Or did he? The result does not ring quite true. The Dyer's Hand has tinged it.

Some days my aura weaker than on others. (A commuter's aura never very strong.) People I know well look straight through me as though I had been minussed. Uncanny feeling of insubstantiality. I smile at acquaintances, even speak to them, and receive no response. Little daily deaths of fear. An unburied shade desperately trying to attract attention.

Crane swinging enormous ball on chain to demolish building beside railway at Didcot where they used to keep fodder for horses in war (not sure what horses or which war). Straight out of *The Wonder Book for Boys*. Bet it was full of rats. The Quartermaster's Stores. My eyes are dim. I see by glimpses now. I wish I were as in the years of old.

ADLEWHAT? 1
Adlestrop? I don't remember the name.
When high speed trains make unscheduled halts
It's such a bore. They spend millions of pounds
And still can't stop them developing faults.

Absent-mindedly strolling along Oxford platform whistling Chattanooga Choo Choo. Guard leans out of van and calls to me: 'Wrong one, sir. This train doesn't stop there.'

Pantechnicon parked on waste ground outside Didcot. On its side, in big ghoulish letters dripping gouts of red paint, GHOST TRAIN . Bats, skeletons, vampires too. Pah! Junior league! Nursery slopes! Peanuts! We can outspook any fairground ghost-train. Roll up! Roll up! For an exorbitant entry fee we offer you a haunting experience. Travel with revenants! Rub shoulder-bones with the living dead! Hear our chains rattle! See our glazed eyes, emaciated features and fearful rictus! Listen to the genuine death râle! Thrills! Thrills! Thrills!

J. tells me he'll spend four weeks' annual leave building an extension to his house. 'I'll save at least £3000,' he says. He expresses horror when I admit to paying a man to put up my bookshelves. I plan to spend a meagre week of my holiday working on Notebook, my equivalent of J.'s extension. My masonry cannot match his, but I might save something. My life, perhaps.

Your Name Could Be Here. (Count yourself blessed if it is not.) Some of those who have helped to make the going that much easier:

Lionel	Walter	Anne	Robin	Martin F.
Alec	Sue	Rabin	Vernon	John D.
John W.	Nick	Judith	Danby	David B.
David J.	Tony D.	Bridgie	Roger	James T.
Paul	Adrian	Keith	Emma	Dimitris
Ruth	David H.	Barry	Frank	Francis
Peter S.	Sheila	Peter C.	Harry	Brian
Denys	Richard C.	Harold	Martin H.	Mike
Vicky	Julian	Mari	Humphrey	Janet
Patrick B.	John R.	Ann	James C.	Wesley
Richard B.	Richard M.	Patrick M.	Tony W.	Quentin
Hugo	Jeremy	Michael	Janice	John F.

Have stopped buying morning paper (only because too dear, not from any lofty principles) and started reading books on train instead. The other day grabbed Malcolm Lowry's *Hear Us O Lord From Heaven Thy Dwelling Place* to re-read. Immediately my mind began to seethe with ideas, over-stimulated by each paragraph. Newspapers never set me going thus. They offer nothing but propaganda deliberately pitched at a level which will not disturb or subvert the nine-to-fivers. Can appreciate why Plato excluded poets, and why totalitarian regimes concentrate so heavily on censorship. Nothing wrong with 'Their' theory. A big book *is*, potentially, a big evil. But 'They' overlook that, in practice, not enough people read books to justify 'Their' efforts. What, after all, have 'They' to fear from a few tired commuters?

Travelled from Oxford to Reading on my season ticket, then changed on to Penzance train. Felt like Alice passing through the looking-glass, or Mary Lennox entering the secret garden. So thin the sheet of glass, the curtain of ivy that separate us from reality. A change of platform, a change of direction, a change of line and, hey presto! the tense commuter becomes a relaxed holidaymaker sharing his small boys' delight in everything from eating crisps in the buffet to riding beside the sea. Such a simple, painless transformation. Life awaits us. Yet day after day we miss the connection.

Uncivil disobedience the order of the day.

To steal the commuters from the railway: the Greatest Train Robbery of all time.

Returning to train after a week's break, greeted by fellow-commuter who says: 'You look relaxed.' Immediate reaction: My God, do I then normally look tense, nervous, haggard, drawn? Suppose I must.

OXFORD STATION 4
IV
Christ Church and Magdalen, Trinity and Balliol,
All Souls and Merton, Blackwell's and
The elephantine Woolworth building
Are all there in a manner of speaking;
They are there in the city and
Here on the platform, for as I alight
It is now and England
Architecture and Oxford
All and nothing.

Arrived at Paddington one hot morning at end of May to find on The Lawn a display of fur coats by a firm with the all-too-apt name of Catman. At other times 'They' try to woo us with double glazing. Both Mr Catman and the window-makers evidently appreciate that the thin blood of commuters renders them more vulnerable to cold than normal human beings. But not clear why they imagine they can check us in our carefully timed run-ins to our offices long enough to sell us their wares. At least we can savour, as we scurry past, the free exhibition of surrealist art – wardrobes without front, back or sides, windows without walls – all standing naked in the open air.

OVERHEARD 19
'I do hope we're not going to have another of those horrible hot summers that go on for months and months and months.'

If you look carefully, you can see traces of the old regime before the coup. The huge letters GWR on the side of the building on your left as you enter Paddington from Praed

Street. Old lavatory buckets put to a variety of uses. Wrought-iron GWR monograms supporting seats, or carved ones surmounting doorways. A luggage trolley at Oxford with the name Abingdon still legible on its side. The word 'Great' painted over on some of the old cast-iron notices. 12-hour clocks (the Revolution imposed the 24-hour system). Blood-stains on floors. Bullet-holes in plaster. Silent, limping veterans with expressionless faces. The safeguard of the West has fallen.

> Men are we, and must grieve when even the Shade
> Of that which once was great is passed away.
> (Wordsworth)

ANTI-KONTAKION 28

A curse on the train. Necromantic Nekuia. Hidden Hades. Malevolent Malebolge. Avernus adit. *Epitome of Erebus. Likeness of Lethe. Shadow of Sheol. Type of Tophet.* Anathema sit.

Note for social historians. One woman gets on at Didcot without her face, and spends most of journey in lavatory putting it on. She emerges wearing a mask out of Japanese drama. Noh thank you. Another, younger, scorns to seek privacy. She produces a metal tool-box containing layers of trays full of lotions, lipsticks, powders, false eyelashes, mascara, tweezers, brushes, scissors etc. etc., and performs a precision engineering job on her face in full view of us all. I admire her steady hands, but long to ask her why she does it.

HEADLINE 12
Woman Injured In Nettlebed Crash.

ADLEWHAT? 2
It was hot, you say? I've no idea –
Rolling-stock's air-conditioned these days,
And the weather always seems threatening
Through tinted glass and double glaze.

Jotted a query: Wm. Burroughs a P.N. man? The answer is no. Take James Joyce, Samuel Beckett, John Berger, Ann

Quin, Aidan Higgins, Anthony Burgess, Charles Haldeman – any writer hailed as an innovator, experimenter, breaker of new ground – and what do you find? They all turn out to be good, old-fashioned novelists, concerned in one way or another to tell a story. True originals are not those who think of new ways of playing old games, but those who invent new games. Not, of course, that originality *per se* constitutes a virtue. But at least it offers a starting-point.

From *Radio Times*:

Harvesting the Dead. Medical technology can now keep a human body 'functioning', even though the brain may be dead. Do we now have a new category of existence – the neomort – whose thinking brain is dead, yet whose heart and lungs are working normally?

No. Neomorts have existed on trains for a good hundred years now. All that medical technology has done is supply a beautiful, new, albeit hybrid word to describe the spent commuter.

A dubious advantage of being rolled round in earth's diurnal course with rocks and stones and trains – you come back to things, or things come back to you. One day D. and I realised we were repeating a conversation we had had six months before. D. delighted because he suddenly understood a cryptic note which he had made on the previous occasion and which had been puzzling him ever since.

Commuters nicely fulfil many of Aristotle's requirements for tragedy. Our condition imitates life (*mimesis*), and fearful and pitiful life at that. True, most of us cannot claim noble or illustrious birth, but otherwise we conform to the definition of the tragic protagonist: 'a man not pre-eminently virtuous and just, whose misfortune is brought upon him not by vice and depravity but by some flaw (*hamartia*)'. This flaw – laziness, avarice, a poor degree, a refusal to face reality, a tendency to drift – has imposed on each of us the reversal of fortune (*peripeteia*) which has placed us on the train. The recognition (*anagnorisis*) comes if and when the scales fall from our eyes and we realise the full horror of our plight. Tragedy aims to effect *katharsis* or purgation. Commuting certainly does this. But Aristotle saw ancient tragedy as purging the emotions of the spectators. Our tragedy has no spectators – except ourselves. We are *spectatores ab intra* of our own tragedy, actors and onlookers. A new concept in audience participation. We have excellent seats. Finally, Aristotle reminds us, a happy ending spoils the drama.

Nous sommes trop pressés pour trouver le lieu et la formule. Always moving on. We are getting the refugee habit. Exiles. Expatriates. Displaced persons. Stateless. What Greeks call 'the unknown ones'. Dear Greece!

'Misspent youth': expression coined by commuters to justify the way we misspend the rest of our lives.

June heatwave. Woman beside me on 1715 had thermometer which reached 100° in the shade. (Perfect example of kind of fatuous item I have done my best to exclude from Notebook.)

Train: a novel, fiction. We: characters. A long, boring *roman-fleuve*. Also a *roman-à-clef* with two-dimensional figures based on real people. We have as much existence as 'They' see fit to allow us. Bradleian question: Is there life beyond the train?

R-U A CO-OPERATOR? IF NOT WHY NOT? Huge old lettering on side of house at Reading. Prompts reflection that to commute is tantamount to co-operating and collaborating with the enemy. *Nous sommes des collabos.* R-U A COMMUTER? IF SO WHY?

HEADLINE 13
Man Did Not Throw Brick.

Due To A Blockade Between
Banbury And Leamington

Found this obsolete, alarming, chalked announcement among a stack of boards with other notices in bike-shed at Oxford. Evidently they use a new board whenever possible rather than erase old gems. Do they beguile wet winter evenings with them?

'Hey, Abdul, let's have another look at that urgent message for Madame Arditti.'

'Pass me the one that says: No Boats Today. That puzzled 'em, didn't it, Arthur?'

'Certainly did. How were they to know it meant the Stranraer–Larne ferry? Remember this one, Abdul – We Are Sorry If The Exteriors Of Our Coaches Are Dirty This Is Due To The Water Shortage?'

Collapse of Abdul and Arthur, laughing helplessly as rain buckets down.

This Notebook not autobiography but autopsy. Am trying to conduct my own *post-mortem*. To write the story of my death.

Lavatory pans on train usually Twyford's 'Envoy', marked Vitreous China. Warped pleasure of peeing into this – but not, of course, flushing it – as we pass through Twyford. Why 'Envoy'? Because *chargé d'affaires*? Surely not. Perhaps its namers had in mind 'the action of dispatching a messenger or parcel'. 'Vitreous' basically means 'glassy', a nice word that deserves to be rescued from lavatory bowls and restored to general circulation: e.g.: He had the vitreous look of a tired commuter . . .

ADLEWHAT? 3
Haycocks and meadowsweet? I wouldn't know.
I never looked outside the train,
Just drank canned beer from a plastic cup
Until the damned thing started again.

Remember spending a chunk of my 21st birthday in a train, returning from a croquet tournament at Budleigh Salterton.

Drank Guinness in the buffet and felt totally content. Little did I know. Time means nothing to the train. It let me have my fling. It waited eleven years before claiming the soul I unwittingly sold in a moment of carefree happiness.

Commuter psychology. When temperature *drops* from 90s to 70s no one opens windows. When it *rises* to 70s people rush to let in as much air as possible.

The nearer you approach to London, the harder everything and everyone find it to resist the centripetal attraction of the metropolis. Witness the fact that the down platforms of Langley, Iver, West Drayton, Hanwell, Hayes are grass-grown and neglected. Some stations have abolished their down platforms altogether.

All too easy to accelerate away from the gravitational pull of Oxford, coast through the outer space of Reading, and enter the magnetic field of London. All too difficult to make the journey in reverse. Few have boosters powerful enough. We took the railroad more travelled by, and that has made all the indifference.

ANTI-KONTAKION 29

A curse on the train. Drudge destroying Isambard's dreams. Sludge silting up immortality's gleams. Terra incognita. Terra non firma. *Repressor of merit. Suppressor of spirit. Mind-muffler. Soul-snuffer.* Anathema sit.

Train offers excellent conditions for studying people asleep. In normal life you see only your nearest and dearest as they slumber. Train provides an anthology of sleepers, from babies to businessmen, from pretty girls to old harridans. Curious phenomenon that sleep seems to beautify the unattractive, but make the attractive ugly. It certainly presents everybody in a different light. It allows you to scrutinise somebody's features, to indulge the voyeur in yourself as you do in front of a television screen. You think: 'How benevolent and placid that noisy, intolerant lawyer looks'; or: 'I wouldn't want to sleep with *her*.'

Smiling also transforms commuters. Many of us wear

special fixed train expressions, to avoid lapsing into face-crime. We scowl, sulk, lower, frown, grimace, snarl, brood. We cultivate an air of permanent anger or sadness, melancholy or hostility. We defy people to sit by us, speak to us, touch us. We distrust the world. But catch us with our guard down – perhaps because we've had a couple of beers, or because our wife or mistress (and not together!) happens to have caught our train – catch us animated or smiling or laughing even, and you will be amazed at our resemblance to ordinary human beings.

Train = worm, in all senses. Worm that feeds on corpses. Worm-monster. Worm-devil. Laley worm. Visible worm that flies in the day and does our life destroy. Wriggling worm concealing the fatal hook. Break it into sections, and each regenerates itself like a Hydra's head. Impassively industrious. Unerringly blind. Reproducing itself in a joyless, sexless way. Useful – necessary, even – and repulsive.

J. points to T., another commuter, and comments critically: 'He's an eccentric, isn't he? If he was a colleague I wouldn't place much confidence in his decisions; would you?' Surprised at J.'s vehemence, I question this. T.'s 'eccentricity' consists in engaging strangers in loud conversation on topics like the character of Richard III or the weaknesses of the British Raj in India, reading serious hardback books, wearing a cloth cap, and carrying a hold-all containing a thermos, a week's supply of cake and a bright yellow scarf. On the train such deviations suffice to brand a man as eccentric.

Put it to J. that many of us are much more eccentric inwardly than T. is outwardly. P., for example, spent several journeys writing an epic in heroic couplets about piles. What reliance would J. place on my judgement if he knew what goes on in my head, some of which finds its way into Notebook? The train likes people to conform, to display grey suits and grey minds. It trainwashes nice people like J. to accept this, but freaks like T., P., and myself will not succumb so easily.

TRACKSIDE INDUSTRY 12
New Dimension Warehouse Shopping Centre. What new dimension?

Interesting to note that 'They' often place First Class coaches at front of train where passengers must walk further to reach them and take the brunt of fumes and noise.

Story of undergraduate convinced that he had performed brilliantly in his examinations. Later the examiners broke it to him that he had done nothing but write his own name over and over again. Be warned, Tiresias!

Peter Parker now in charge of British Rail. Not much he will need to be told about webs and networks. Cf. Pope:

> The spider's touch, now exquisitely fine!
> Feels at each thread, and lives along the line.

Compared myself to Penelope as possibly too scared to face consequences of completing my work. Had forgotten that a) she was weaving a shroud, and b) after three years of nocturnal unpicking she was betrayed and obliged to finish. As for a), nothing wrong in preparing shrouds – one's own or others' – in good time. As for b), I have already managed to penelopize for much longer than she did.

T.S. Eliot can certainly claim title Poet of Commuting, if not Commuter Poet. Not only specific images: the crowd flowing over London Bridge, the world moving on its metalled ways, the underground train stopping too long between stations, the narrowing rails sliding together, but also the whole ethos of *The Waste Land* and *Four Quartets* bespeak commuterdom. Here is a place of disaffection. I too have sat by Thebes below the wall in my green unknowing youth – not such a bad place to be.

Exception to Grecian Urn Syndrome: combine harvester clanks round decreasing wheat. Old man with gun cocked stands waiting. Rabbit dashes past him on blind side and escapes over stubble. Old man remains unmoving. Whole episode witnessed from train in flash.

OVERHEARD 20

Woman to man on early train: 'May I borrow your Times*? I don't feel up to* The Lancet *yet.'*

ADLEWHAT? 4

A blackbird sang? Look, where've you been?
Modern coaches are sound-proof, see;
All I could hear was the guard on the tannoy
Somewhere in Area Thirty-Three.

One morning on Oxford Station met some neighbours setting off for walking holiday.

'And you do this every day?' says wife. 'It must be very tiring.'

Husband chips in: 'But he looks very well on it.'

Ah, the inner anguish does not show. The ordeal leaves few outward marks. Quote from the commission's report: 'We could find no evidence of torture or violation of human rights.'

TRACKSIDE INDUSTRY 13

Accident Repair Specialists. How do you repair an accident?

Possible best-selling sequels to Notebook: *Confessions of a Commuter, The Day of the Commuter, Onward Virgin Commuters, It Shouldn't Happen to a Commuter, The Commuter Who Came in from the Train.* I'm on to a winning streak all right.

DIALOGUE 10

J.: *'When I went to renew my season ticket, the man at the ticket office recognised me.'*
Self: *'How nice.'*
J.: *'It's not nice. It's bloody depressing.'*

Poster: Children For Only 25p Each – Prices Slashed!

D. acquired some shirts made from cabbage (illegal trimmings) and peddled them discreetly on the train. I bought one. – The pathetically small railway bazaar.

OVERHEARD 21

'It wasn't a breakdown or a signal failure. Everything just got stuck at Maidenhead.'

Sometimes when we arrive at Oxford, announcer advises: 'Passengers for Kingham please travel in centre of the train.' Try saying this fast, especially with Asian accent. Always expect everyone to blush scarlet or stop dead in their tracks. But they never do.

ANTI-KONTAKION 30

A curse on the train. Strappado. Bastinado. Castigator. Mad dictator. Flagellator. Inquisitor's torture. Scavenger's daughter. Anathema sit.

Trapped thistledown: paradigm of seed that falls, like us, on barren ground.

Whiteness of snow blankets sleeping seed. Whiteness of blossom fulfils winter faith. Whiteness of drought negates everything – bleached bone, whited sepulchre. Whiteness of harvest the answer to prayer. Mine, O thou lord of life, send my roots rain, but even more, send my branches sun.

Oxford Station, 0700. Tannoy breaks silence: 'Passenger coming along to the bay for the Malvern train.' Brave, anadromous souls travelling against the flow – so rare that they announce them individually, with pride. 'One unperforated Penny Black!'

TRAIN GAME 9 and MYSTERY 14

Like to try to place fellow-passengers. May often go wildly wrong, but at least most of them invite interesting hypotheses, some of which are confirmed or contradicted in due course. Have had fun speculating about the cigar-smoking Jewess, the over-laden librarian, the cycling toff, and others. But have to admit myself completely stymied by a newcomer. Even its sex remains indeterminate. Of small stature, youngish, dumpy, with medium-length dark hair, it wears a loose-fitting windcheater and baggy trousers. It arrives at the station astride a huge motor-bike, short legs scarcely able to touch ground. It plays the fruit machine in the waiting-room. It smokes. It moves serenely on its way, the suspicion of an inscrutable smile playing on its hermaphrodite lips.

Terminus. For Romans a deity, the *numen* of boundary-marks set up with sacrifice and fire. A Terminus had to stand under open sky; if incorporated into a building an opening had to be left in roof – cf. Paddington where vents allow some air (not to mention rain and snow) to enter and some fumes to escape. Can mean finishing-point or starting-point. The end is where we start from. But we must start soon, because doctrine of terminism teaches that we all have only a limited term for repentance.

KEY to LOOSE COUPLING 1
A lisping bLONDON PADDINGTON
Showed girls his ROYAL OAK,
One left the train at WESTBOURNE PARK,
Would not ACTON his joke.

Nous sommes les amortis.

Young American man passed a journey embroidering with coloured wools the text: *Non Est Carborundum.*

Feel more akin to poets than to prose-writers. These notes a collection of poems fortuitously bound together. Their interreaction and cumulative effect beyond my control. They appear (except for some items like Obit, Anti-kontakion, Loose Coupling etc.) in order they were written, but can be read in any order. Most books of poetry, however, repay that which they seldom receive, a reading from cover to cover, in process of which emerge perspectives undreamt of by the poet. May this also prove true of Notebook.

From an official printed British Rail poster advertising Windsor:

Runnymede
A fine expanse of riverside

174

> meadow at the foot of
> Coopers Hill. Nearby are the
> John F. Kennedy and Magna
> Carter memorials.

Was Magna Carter a daughter of the revolution and ancestress of Jimmy, or simply the man who delivered champagne to the castle on a horse-drawn dray?

We grow dangerously dependent on the train – schizophrenics habituated to their asylum. If discharged, could we any longer cope with ordinary life? Awful possibility that we could not survive for long away from our padded cells.

RAF commuter calls little local stopping trains 'puddle-jumpers'.

Doyen of Oxford commuters alleged to have been making the trip for over thirty years, and to spend his journeys munching celery, lettuce, water-cress, carrots, apples etc. Don't know where he lurks, but like the idea of a ghostly rabbit as king of the commuters.

Wisdom of poor Eugene Lee-Hamilton, whose sonnet *Sunken Gold* says it all:

> In dim green depths rot ingot-laden ships,
>> While gold doubloons that from the drowned hand fell
>> Lie nestled in the ocean's flower bell
> With Love's gemmed rings once kissed by now dead lips.
> And round some wrought-gold cup the sea-grass whips
>> And hides lost pearls, near pearls still in their shell,
>> Where seaweed forests fill each ocean dell,
> And seek dim sunlight with their countless tips.
>
> So lie the wasted gifts, the long-lost hopes,
>> Beneath the now hushed surface of myself,
> In lonelier depths than where the diver gropes
>>> They lie deep, deep; but I at times behold
>> In doubtful glimpses, on some reefy shelf,
>>> The gleam of irrecoverable gold.

Notice in buffet about what to do 'when car is stabled at night'.

Proverb: You cannot put old commuters in new trains.

Est-ce que c'est un carnet intime?

Observing Goring-Pangbourne-Tilehurst crowd, have noticed pairs who are clearly father and son. I find this absolutely terrifying.

ANTI-KONTAKION 31
A curse on the train. Isolater. Insulator. Capsule. Module. Hell-car. Bell-jar. Too secure womb. Premature tomb. Atmosphere coming between us and reality. Bathysphere plumbing unseen depths of banality. Anathema sit.

J., fighting way on to train: 'That's what God gave me big shoulders for – so that I could commute in peace.'

KEY TO LOOSE COUPLING 2
He pleaded quite appEALINGly,
More clumsily tHANWELL,
But had no wELTHORNEoble blood,
So she ran off pell-mell.

Line from John Berryman: 'We must travel in the direction of our fear.' Commuters bear this out – but absolutely no reason why we should accept it.

Dew-drenched grass seen through train window in October – desirable, untouchable, moist pubic hair.

MYSTERY 15
Over a long period, when 1715 arrived from carriage sidings in the evenings it would bring, scowling from one of the windows, a young satyr, looking like an elf who had lost his beads.

J.'s wife left him for another man. Divorce proceedings had been instigated. He still saved the marriage by giving up commuting. An Orpheus who regained his Eurydice by leaving the underworld and not looking back.

A., coming up behind me on platform: 'Ah, I'd know that stance anywhere.' It had never occurred to me before that I had a recognisable stance. Encouraging to know that one can still be identified in the waiting crowd.

DIALOGUE 11

A. again, as we braced ourselves for Tilehurst invasion: 'Here come the motley crew.'
Self: 'That's just what they're not. They're a monochrome crew.'

When the inspector doesn't bother you for your ticket; when you find yourself only person in full coach who knows how to switch on lights; when the guard opens the door for you; when the buffet attendant knows your order in advance; when the paper lady (bless her) gives you credit and asks if you've had a good holiday; when 'They' offer you classes in Art Appreciation on the 0714; when you prefer to sit down to wait for the train; when a rowdy group of young commuters (one of whom strangely resembles yourself six years ago) irritates you; – all these are signs that you have outlived your time and should quit. In fact you should have quitted the minute you began to commute.

TRACKSIDE INDUSTRY 14

Stopping by works on a rainy evening. Sign says: Works Entrance. And so they do. Entrance the beholder, I mean. Especially in this case when, through iron railings festooned with raindrops, we regard Sir Erich Pasold's factory with its unashamedly whimsy picture of ladybirds spinning, and with huge jolly replicas of the red and black insects clamped to the walls. A pleasantly lachrymose and coleopterous sight.

My first lustre has passed. In that time I have seen the flower of Oxford's youth turn grey, careworn and middle-aged. I have tempted the Fates by neglecting the prescribed purificatory sacrifice. May this Notebook appease them.

Gordon, old fruit, where are you? Are you receiving me? Roger. Come in, come in. I need you to help me recover my footing on my Theban hill, and to cock snooks at *Schicksal* and *Verhängnis*. Bring your victory-bearing, enormous snot-rag. Remember, *Denken ist Luxus*.

As for you, Paul, I know where you are, and that gives me strength and reassurance. You with your poems and girls. Me with my prose and verse. Let's concoct an entry for the Event of the Year Competition. Eh, old horse?

Distinguished searching man tried to stand his executive case upright on overhead luggage rack. It wouldn't go, of course. He should know by now. This the only occasion when I've been able to watch him in the act of sitting down. A marbled murrelet stalked to its nest.

OVERHEAD 22
'All there was was the airstrip in, the hotel, and these temples cut out of the jungle – it was real India.'

KEY TO LOOSE COUPLING 3
As he went west, the girl went SOUTH
ALL flustered in a HAYES,
While HARLINGTONs of oaths at him
Which left him in a daze.

A perfect moment, no matter what happens next. No matter that tomorrow is Friday the 13th. October heatwave. Reclining in ex-First Class Parker Knoll type *fauteuil* No 19 on 1800. Working inside me, a pint of Paddington Bass. (A consolation of approaching middle age – it takes less alcohol to do the trick.) Riding off, saddle ablaze, into sunset. 'I always expect the angels to pee into my beer,' enigmatically remarks *mon cher* Henry Miller. Feel as delicately critical as gelignite. Yes. This is it.

Satan, according to Book of Job, spends his time 'going to and fro'. In perambulation and peripateticism, with their connotations of aimlessness, pleasure, creativity, lies virtue. Likewise the akinesis of a Buddha under a bo tree has much to recommend it. But in going to and fro, day after day, along a rigid, inflexible course, commuters delight the devil and become his instruments. We don't even sell our souls. We lack the wit of Faustus. No temporary omniscience for us. No phantom embraces from Miss Universe. We strike no bargain, we just surrender unconditionally. And Old Nick chortles all the way back to Hellacious Acres.

Didcot notice (white on red):

> Warning Do Not Cross The Line
> Whilst Shunting Is In Progress

Sometimes we see the shunters walking behind wagons with their mysterious poles. More sinister than cowled nomadic shepherds. They look more like fiends from Dante. Best to take the warning seriously.

Suddenly remembered Thomas Traherne. His *Centuries of Meditations* constitute without doubt the greatest and archetypal Premeditated Notebook. Even Palinurus must grovel before him.

An empty book is like an infant's soul, in which anything may be written. It is capable of all things, but containeth nothing. I have a mind to fill this with profitable wonders.

What enviable confidence — totally justified. Profitable wonders! Traherne filled page after page with them, never faltering in style or tone. He makes me feel ashamed. With its unprofitable commonplaces, my Notebook represents the death-throes of a decadent genre.

ANTI-KONTAKION 32
A curse on the train. Joiner of that which should not be joined. Sunderer of that which should not be sundered. Communications system symbolising non-communication. Conveyance conveying nothing. Anathema sit.

14 February. Mild, springlike. I ache. Suffering from impacted sap. The ascending juyce, not readily passing, settles in knots and inequalities.

Approaching Paddington – a Spiderman skyscape.

Train resembles airliner. Obviously it has fuselage, under-carriage, cabin, cockpit, pilot, passengers etc. Inside it we feel the detachment of airborne travellers, strive to suppress our fear of flying. It sways, banks, hits turbulence and airpockets. Adverse weather conditions (one of announcers' stock phrases) affect it. It sustains unexplained bumps and jolts. Sometimes it seems to loiter to use up fuel. Sometimes it waits outside station in a stack. When train does come in, the landing can be rough or smooth. Just one main difference, it never takes off – a flight-simulator, not the real thing.

Tangram man produces from his attaché case sheets of Civil Service paper with royal arms at top, prepared grids, and a box of coloured plastic shapes. He spends hours producing permutations and noting each one down, whis-tling as he works.

OVERHEARD 23
'I've been to the Scilly Isles several times.'
'Oh, did you run into Harold Wilson?'
'I rubbed shoulders with him once in the Co-op.'

I have become the train. *Le train, c'est moi.* No longer the child who says: 'Look, Daddy, I'm a puffer train.' Not make-believe, but sur-reality.

Anyone crazy enough to film Notebook would have to hire a Hollywood expert to animate commuters.

Same satisfaction from solving *The Times* crossword as from ravelling out a difficult poem. Crossword tantamount to a form of poetry.

Battles for lower fares, faster trains, better services, all irrelevant. We want out. Only one battle – the battle for release.

KEY TO LOOSE COUPLING 4
Alone in his compartment, he
WEST DRAYTONing his dress,
When 'Will YIEWSLEYp with me?' inquired
A winsome Scottish lass.

Notebook ought to be printed in facsimile, for the handwriting itself tells story as well as the words. Confident and insouciant to start with, it has become increasingly crabbed and shaky over the years. Like the journal of a doomed explorer it betrays decrepitude moving inexorably towards the one event which the writer himself cannot record.

MYSTERY 17
Paddington announcement in broad daylight: 'Will the station lampman please take two lamps to platforms 8 and 9.' Had message taken light years to arrive?

Woods used in construction of spacious old First Class carriages, named on proud labels: Eucalyptus, Australia; Eucalyptus, California; Crown Elm, England; Lacewood, England; Sapele, West Africa; Zebrano, Brazil.

Early Morning in Winter
Yellow, steamed-up railway vans
Parked beside cold marshalling-yards:
Men with chipped white billy-cans
Drinking tea and playing cards.

Duffle-hooded track-maintenance men, out in all weathers, look like Vlach shepherds. They subsist in a different time-scale from ours. Wordsworthian figures who pace about the weary rails continually.

'The journey, not the arrival, matters.' Leonard Woolf apparently found this in Montaigne. Did Stevenson know of it? Our journey certainly does not matter. What matters is that we should cease to make it. 'Is your journey really necessary?' No – totally unnecessary. Only when we have stopped commuting can we begin to make journeys that matter, *beaux voyages (comme Ulysse)*, travels full of hope.

A commuter the complete opposite of Ulysses/Odysseus. We have never made a voyage in our lives. Voyage comes from *voir* and means 'a seeing'. For all the thousands of miles we have covered, we have *seen* nothing. We could have seen much more by staying at home. Our voyage will only begin when we reach a place where the natives take our briefcases for ditty-bags and our season tickets for mermaids' purses.

Curious how long-dormant scraps of French keep rising to surface. Suppose because French *par excellence* language of mood and tone of Notebook, i.e. of wistfulness and nostalgia with a dash of surrealism; of search for *temps perdu;* of *déjà vu;* of *double entendre;* of *ennui, cafard, canard;* of *chemin de fer;* of *si vieillesse savait, si jeunesse pouvait* (sic). *Le vent se lève. Allons enfants!*

ANTI-KONTAKION 33
A curse on the train. Frankenstein meddling with genetics. Wittgenstein fiddling with semantics. Metaphorical process. Allegorical progress. Locus of tedium. Focus for odium. Anathema sit.

A cold January night. I got up and closed window. Middle European type jumped to his feet, flung window open again, and yelled at me: 'In future don't behave like a jackboot.'

OVERHEARD 24
'If you can't trust a map, what can you trust?'

> The beauty of a fog or haze
> Is redoubled for the mind
> That has glimpsed on clearer days
> Realities that lie behind.

When the latest kind of train slows down, odour of brake fluid enters the air-conditioning system, making smell as though all passengers – except the sniffer – have been eating oranges.

KEY TO LOOSE COUPLING 5
'For IVER yen for a lang, LANGLEY,
Look, mon, my bra I SLOUGH,
As for my panties, bide a wee
And I will BURNHAM now!'

Chilterns and Berkshire Downs look Greek one day, Scottish another, Chinese the next.

From *Concise Oxford Dictionary*: '**passenger** (colloq.) member of team, crew etc., who does, or can do, no effective work'.

Graffito near Paddington, June 1977: A POX ON THE JUBILEE: THE ERSATZ ORGASM OF THE SILENT MAJORITY. Frightfully embarrassing. How fortunate for everyone that the silent majority rapidly painted it out.

The train turns to dross all that it touches. It warps, twists, parodies, distorts everything, from human beings to philosophical theories. 'Only connect' makes nonsense – 'only disconnect' becomes the rule of the train. Bergson's *élan* changes from *vital* to *mortel*. The meaning of meaning grows meaningless. Felt life = unfelt death. Superman turns subhuman. Illogical negativism and unregenerate grammar prevail. Relativity has nothing to relate to. Faith doubts. Hope despairs. Love sleeps under a general anaesthetic.

OVERHEARD 25
'And in the end the bank manager died at Christmas, and that solved my problem, because the new manager had a much more flexible approach.'

Reading *Selected Poems* of Norman Nicholson on train. 'Yellow surf of stonecrop', he writes. I glance out of window and there it is, sprawling over coaldust and clinkers. I turn the page and next poem begins: 'The last clinkers of sunset . . .' Such juxtaposition unlikely to recur this side the tomb.

OXFORD STATION 5
V

I trod the pavement in a dead patrol
While, leaves swept by the scuttling wind,
Grasping their soiled tickets in readiness,
Obols for Charon, three fellow-travellers
Progressed towards the uncertain distance
At the recurrent end of the unending –
Where I beheld an uncouth shape,
I could also ken that he was clothed
In the garb of a railway official,
Though faded, yet entire,
Although I was not really there and knew
Also that he did not exist,
My words would only crack beneath the strain
Of the attempt to make him understand
This double state of being and non-being.
So I assumed audacity and said
To the man who stood at the gate:
'I have lost my ticket,
What are you going to do?'
In few plain words he answered my predicament
In language such as I could comprehend:
'You have to go in by the way you go in,
You have to go out by the way you go out,
The way in is the way out,
The way out is the way in,
In between there is no other way,
Only the entrance and the exit,
And the entrance and the exit are the same
With nothing in between,
With nothing in between.'

Acolyte women tiptoe and tittup into supervisor's sanctum like their churchy counterparts who attend early mass, arrange the flowers, and pursue the vicar into the vestry.

Some carriages have panel over door which lights up whenever anyone bolts themselves into the lavatory. A useful aid to the male imagination. When a pretty girl leaves her seat, the light tells us she has not gone to the buffet. When light goes out, we can brace ourselves for her return.

OVERHEARD 26

'I built a spiral staircase out of brick with a nine-foot diameter central drum, with an archway set in it. Though I say it myself, it's a very fine thing.'

Train wheels gride on rails and in our hearts.

Delay ascribed to 'congestion at Didcot'.

Train: a snake that hypnotises its prey, a boa constrictor that crushes life out of its victims, a python that swallows commuters whole.

KEY TO LOOSE COUPLING 6

'TAPLOW my MAIDENHEAD,' she begged.
'I'll TWYFORDevilwy,'
Our hero lisped, and very soon
Was tREADING manfully.

Or again, the train is like the old Court of Chancery. Its suitors cannot withstand its fascination, cannot absent themselves. They waste away, led on by false hopes of a judgement in their favour, which never comes.

ANTI-KONTAKION 34

A curse on the train. Enemy of promise. Enema and vomit. Vehicle in which we precariously move. Cubicle in which we vicariously live. Punishment. Banishment. Violator of valleys. Vitiator of values. Anathema sit.

Sudden realisation: fences and walls by railway not to discourage trespassers, but to prevent us from escaping.

They flee from me who sometime did me seek, stomping with well-shod feet in my compartment.

Train: a maggot in the cosmic apple.

Ticket-collectors on the new trains walk up and down like Diogenes, calling out: 'Didcot joiners, Didcot joiners'. Cannot imagine anyone else recording such a detail if I do not.

Courteous pair of older Oxford commuters, after I had nipped smartly aboard crowded train: 'We must congratulate you on your energetic sprint – most excellent.'

The interiors of the new trains, with harsh lights and conditioned air, resemble television studios. Staff and passengers respond to the artificial setting by acting like people on set. They affect exaggerated fixed smiles and false bright conversation of commercials. Cameras whirr. Reels revolve. Behind the celluloid lie the abyss, panic and emptiness.

Gabriel, my friend, what is all this if not Lego?

MYSTERY 18
Heard over tannoy at Paddington: 'Staff announcement: the 1540 workerbus is a locomotive from the parcels line.' Evidence to support theory of existence of at least one other world coterminous with ours. We call it ours, but ants, badgers, birds, fairies, workerbuses, ghosts, may also call it theirs, and see us as intruders making use of their tracks, paths, airways, rails, space. Every now and then the curtain fleetingly parts. One day perhaps we shall discover the underground railroad where sympathetic conductors wait to guide escaped commuters to safety.

Train: a chained library of unread books. Or a lost desert cave containing mouldering scrolls of wisdom.

OVERHEARD 27
Guard on Oxford train making unscheduled stop at Didcot: 'I've got a couple of Readings on here somewhere – they might as well get out now.'

On wireless a prominent Roman Catholic suggested (heretically?) that Jesus possessed two kinds of consciousness – one for heaven and one for earth. Speaker cited the way a person can have a 'home' and an 'office' consciousness, with little or no contact between the two. This improbable theory would make Jesus into a commuter. If true, Christians could abandon all hope straight away. A commuting God could not possibly save the world. All the same, interesting to speculate on what sort of service exists between Paradise and Kensal Green, or Heaven and Charing Cross.

Despite what cynics may allege, usually the train goes very fast. This makes observing the passing scene like trying to read label on a revolving gramophone record. Each time we decipher a little more and store it in our memory-banks. Thus, when we look out of window at any given moment, much of what we think we are seeing we are in fact remembering. Just as in conversation we supply half of what we believe we are hearing.

Knotebook – a knotted net to hold my luggage; or an escape rope knotted together from the contents of my ragbag mind. But will they take the strain?

KEY TO LOOSE COUPLING 7
'How tacTILEHURSTrong fingers are!
How sweet her PANGBOURNE cries!'
He mused, while GORING with a will
On her train-shaken thighs.

Interesting for a truck-spotter to find this in Humphrey Carpenter's excellent Tolkien biography:

Yet the railway cutting had grass slopes, and here he (Tolkien) discovered flowers and plants. And something else attracted his attention: the curious names on the coal-trucks in the sidings below, odd names which he did not know how to pronounce but which had a strange appeal to him. So it came about that by pondering over *Nantyglo*, *Senghenydd*, *Blaen-Rhondda*, *Penrhiwceiber*, and *Tredegar*, he discovered the existence of the Welsh language.

I seem to recall something similar too in Louis MacNeice's autobiography *The Strings are False*. Engine-numbers take you nowhere, but truck-inscriptions serve as starting-posts towards all the two and thirty palaces.

TRACKSIDE INDUSTRY 15
Big sign has appeared near Old Oak Common: Ferrous Fragmentisers. Could it conceal what used to be called a breaker's yard?

Another old shikari's trick: pushing socks down to discourage ankles from swelling.

Whiff of revolution: 'British Rail apologise for the delay which was due to the removal of the First Class coach.'

Someone has coined expression 'circadian dysrhythmia' to describe jet-lag. That's nothing. Commuters suffer from train-lag or quotidian dysrhythmia.

All these years – I now realise – I have been subconsciously shying away from idea of train as phallic symbol. But of course that is what it is before all else; which makes us, the passengers, insignificant spermatozoa, mostly spilled on the ground, of which only one or two will ever become human beings.

By the same token, how could I have omitted to mention that we run for several miles of our journey – not long after passing Maidenhead – through Middlesex?

Again, the train is a greenhouse used for experiments by a mad gardener. He subjects us to extremes of temperature. He deprives us of air and moisture. He plants us too close to one another. Gleefully he watches us struggle and wither. Few mature and bear fruit.

ANTI-KONTAKION 35
A curse on the train. Cover for ornithologists. Hide for anthropologists. Dummies' wax museum. Mummies' mausoleum. Dragon. Gorgon. Selector whose votes go to contented sheep. Rejector of goats who unrepentant weep. Anathema sit.

Paddington clock  without hands.

Much more beautiful.

Hands mar the symmetry of time.

Daily we speed along the narrow sixty-mile strip. Our vision stretches so far and no farther. We remain unaware that the vast layout we take so seriously is but a model terminated by abrupt papier mâché cliffs.

So much junk in transit on Oxford platform. We laugh at Victorian catalogues full of quaint inventions, but at least their patent devices had charm and beauty. Packing and dispatching our dull gimmicks and gewgaws seems utterly futile. All that cardboard and plastic. All those international symbols and polyglot instructions which no one reads. One 5 October I spotted a consignment of Sanctuary Lamp Elements travelling with a

> Flame retardant
> 55″ Christmas Cypress Tree
> 2 Tone Green
> Made In Taiwan

O sad cypress . . .

What promise of pneumatic bliss in that expression 'They' use at Paddington: the Bristol end.

The train: an anti-think-tank.

'Will Miss Bennett of Bath please call at the Area Manager's office', has a pleasant Janeite ring to it. Another intriguing announcement: 'Calling Dr Watson, we have a message for you.'

'STREATLEY between oursells,' said she,
'I CHOLSEY what I feel,
So tell me what that MOULSFORDear?'
'For added sex appeal,'
Replied he; she DIDCOTton on
And cried: 'I shall not give
An APPLEFORDecorum now,
However long I live!'

Flash of enlightenment: Paddington Station is *small*. Not the vast, overawing cathedral I used to think it. More of an intimate, roomy parish church with three modest aisles.

Richard Emeny, Emmett Jarrett, Bob Kahan, and Anton Vinogradoff – ideal back-up team for any writer: bibliophile, priest, doctor, and permanent night man – thank you for all your encouragement. And Liz. Oh yes, and Liz, without whom. X.

Between Goring and Tilehurst there seem to be three or four manor-houses visible from the train. 'Seem to be' because, while on some days one or other of them stands out so clearly that you can almost count its mullioned windows, on other days you may only glimpse a ghostly gable or even see nothing at all. Lost domains.

Boarded at Oxford one December morning to find train full of Worcestershire farmers bursting out of their best tweed jackets. They talked loudly and unself-consciously, gesturing with their great hands. One expressed amazement at the sight of concrete sleepers. Another indicated scornfully the enormous unenclosed fields, and commented: 'Not much profit in 'edge-cuttin' round yur.' They all chuckled like children. *Nimis fortunati.*

Commuting psychiatrist explaining how he knew instantly that someone he met at a party also commuted: 'His face had that flat look, if you know what I mean.'

Message chalked on blackboard at Oxford Station:

Mr D.M. EVANS
PLEASE RETURN
TO JESUS.

Moment of crisis for the mysterious patrolling man. An acquaintance with a vacant seat beside him hailed him, inviting him to sit down. He extricated himself with 'I won't come and crowd you and ruin your journey', and passed on.

OVERHEARD 28
'And what do you do with yourself the rest of the year?'
'Oh I run the village newsletter.'

People from Slough with their four-a-side faces.

Was about to write that the Man on the Clapham Omnibus has been superseded by the Man on the London Train. On reflection realise this not true. People used to defer to the former and quote his views. Nobody defers to us. The world at large scarcely knows of our existence, let alone our opinions. But they will. They will.

DIALOGUE 12
1744. Paddington. Platform 1. Signboard announces 1800 due to depart from this platform as usual. SM's in his office. All's right with the world.
1745. Enter a porter, who removes signboard.
Self (fearing worst): 'Does this mean the 6 o'clock isn't leaving from this platform?'
Porter: 'Oh no, sir. But there's no point in putting up the board before the train comes in, is there?'
Collapse of party not very stout in first place.

ANTI-KONTAKION 36
A curse on the train. A and not A train. To be and not to be train. See and not see train. Vasculum. Vacuum. Vivarium. Aquarium. Microbe. Space probe. Fatal and perfidious bark built in th'eclipse. Where men after hideous work wilt and collapse. Anathema sit.

We are the undead, holding out our hands longingly towards the farther platform. – Scribbled that without an idea of what was meant by term 'undead'. Trying to check the word, discovered a conspiracy of silence in dictionaries and encyclopaedias until Webster led me to vampires. So, yet another example of how everything ties up. Odysseus sprinkling trench with blood in order to talk with Tiresias. Nekuia and Ezra Pound. *The Red Limbo Lingo*. Vampires on the ghost train. Anaemia that destroys commuters' red corpuscles. Commuters too passive to be anything but victims. We let others suck our blood, but we do not retaliate.

Christopher Isherwood in *Down There on a Visit*:

the chick has only a limited number of pecks by which to break the shell. The moment that number has been passed, if the chick has failed to break through, it'll begin to weaken and presently suffocate.

OVERHEARD 29
(Outside Oxford Station where, as already noted, a furniture warehouse overlooks the cemetery.) 'It all depends whether you regard the graveyard as a repository or a depository.'

KEY TO LOOSE COUPLING 9
'When girls ask me to CULHAM, I
Do not think of them badly,'
He said; and she: 'I was afeerd
I'd acted ratheRADLEY.'

STILL MORE TRAVELLING TITLES
Foundry Practice. Plank-on-Frame Models. Britain's Greatest Rail Disaster. The Effect of Tyre Deflation on Vehicle Behaviour. Locomotive Practice and Performance. Embryo Transfer in Farm Animals: a review of techniques and applications. Recombinant Molecules. The Paternity of Children Conceived by Artificial Insemination.

Easily the most revolutionary development during my stretch as a commuter has been Big BR's magnanimous decision to allow bicycles to travel free of charge. At a stroke there came into being an inner wheel of the commuting fraternity, the bicycle brigade. We have learned to play a new kind of roulette, gambling on the position of the guard's van, which is never in the same place two days running. We compete for space with day-old chicks, homing pigeons, newspapers, polythene-wrapped girlie magazines, cheeses, Her Majesty's mails, cripples in wheelchairs, motor car parts, undergraduates' trunks, schoolboys' tuck-boxes, and mysterious wooden chests belonging to the railway. We have an uneasy relationship with guards, porters and GPO staff. They are surely justified in resenting the daily invasion of their hitherto inviolate sanctum.

Naturally a special camaraderie exists among us. We enjoy exchanging esoteric anecdotes or discussing the finer points of cycling commuting. One man remarked, on the appearance of a new klaxon on my crossbar: 'I admire its potent position.' Another, explaining why he had bought a new bicycle, said: 'The extravagance was justified by ratiocination.' All very civilised. It gives us an inexhaustible topic for conversation with non-commuters. It adds a welcome new ingredient to our commuting. But it does not alter or alleviate our basic predicament.

Dutch elm disease – the commuter's friend. It has opened up so many views to us, revealed so much that was hidden.

Came across this in Richard Jefferies' *Nature Near London*:

There is a subtle connection between the physical man and the great nature which comes pressing up so closely to the metropolis. He still depends, as in the dim ages before the Pyramids, upon this tiny yellow grain here, rubbed out from the ear of wheat. The clever mechanism of the locomotive which bears him to and fro, week after week and month after month, from home to office and from office to home, has not rendered him in the least degree independent of this.

One of the first attempts at verse I ever made began:

> Serene and sultry in the drowsy morn
> The country station stood –
> One side a field of waving corn,
> The other side a wood.

For the past few years, at least, I have been travelling in the wrong direction. (A commuter, by definition, cannot travel in the right direction.) Now I have to find a way out of the perplex't paths and blind mazes of the drear and tangl'd wood, back to the orient and immortal wheat of childhood on the other side of the tracks. To become fully conscious of my dependence on the tiny yellow grain and to exchange once and for all the clever mechanism of the locomotive for the synagogue of the ear of corn.

Automatic indicator at Oxford flickers through various possibilities: Special, Newcastle, Maidenhead, Terminates Here, Hereford, Excursion, Liverpool, Mystery Tour. It always comes to rest on Paddington. A doctored roulette wheel on which the bank wins every time.

Wish I'd been at Didcot the day the tunnel flooded and a porter played Charon, ferrying passengers from staircase to staircase in a Brute.

Believe it or not, somebody has now written a book called *Coma*. We commuters can buy it in a coma, read it in a coma, and continue on our comatose way.

On stopping trains you can observe the development – or deterioration – of commuters. Each intake from each station is subtly different. Between Oxford and Maidenhead, hair grows greyer, suits darker, faces fatter, mien more serious, and politics bluer.

OVERHEARD 30

He: 'I feel as though I'm committed for every minute of the next two years.'
She: 'Never mind. I can easily change them in Walthamstow.'

Commuter's paradise: a place where a line is a line of verse; a train a train of thought; a station one's station in life; a sleeper someone in bed; a coupling two people in bed; and so on through the whole violated vocabulary.

Spotted passing through Oxford: wagons marked Highly Inflammable – In Emergency Telephone Stockton-on-Tees 553768.

Who am I? I am Banquo in the empty seat. Batteries failing. Signal weak. I am the man who isn't there. At the Christmas pantomime. In church. In the compartment corner. I am the man who does not read *The Cincinnatti Bulletin*. I am the anarchist in the grey suit. I wasn't there again today. I wish to God I'd go away.

People ask why the Second World War produced so few War Poets. They see this as a perfectly natural and legitimate question. They expect poetry to have come out of that hell. It does not even occur to them to demand Commuter Poets. Few know that our hell exists. Fewer still expect to hear from it so much as a lost linnet singing. Commuting and war have this in common – they force people to come out into the open and make their private behaviour public. Cf. Henry Moore's studies of sleeping figures taking refuge from air raids in the Underground. The Government ought to commission Train Artists, for, without some kind of record, posterity will never believe that this huge quiet disaster occurred.

KEY TO LOOSE COUPLING 10
'A pOXFORDecency!' exclaimed
The trouser-buttoning swain;
'I'll second that,' the lass rejoined,
'I'm glad I caught this train!'

Buffers

Il faut reculer pour mieux reculer.

After watching the debouchement from the 1800 one evening, a non-commuting friend declared: 'It looked like the Establishment coming home to dinner.'

OVERHEARD 31
(Snatch from impenetrable talk about diamond lattices and tetrahedra.) 'The value of p and q will depend on the degeneracy of the vibrational state.'

And now to announce the winners of our Biggest Bores Competition. The result is a tie between the man who held forth for an hour on the constitutions of trade unions, and the man who ancient-marinered a complete stranger and expounded to him in detail the workings of his pocket calculator. Late entry, *hors concours*: man who unfolded to his companion plans to make £3 million out of mail order business in 'whole range of contraceptives – jellies, creams, pessaries, diaphragms – the lot'.

ANTI-KONTAKION 37
A curse on the train. Hijacker. Kidnapper. Rapist. Sadist. Terrorist. Hypnotist. Extortioner. Executioner. Depriver of reason. Receiver of ransom. Hostage-maker. Mortgage-taker. Anathema sit.

Most commuters are two-dimensional plywood replicas put there to fool the enemy – who is not fooled for a moment.

Lewis Carroll used to travel by train between Oxford and London armed with a bag full of games, puzzles and other diversions to assist him in chatting up his fellow-passengers, especially small girls. Apparently he enjoyed involving the whole compartment in his amusements. Remarked to a teenage girl of my acquaintance that here was the sort of fellow I would avoid like the plague. She was shocked, saying she'd be delighted to travel in the company of such a lovely man. Once I might have felt the same, but commuting has made me sour and cynical. Even so, I do just wonder how pure Carroll's motives were, and how many rebuffs he suffered . . .

(Cf. John Fuller's sinister sonnet *In a Railway Compartment*.)

People write about situations comparable to ours – e.g. boarding schools, offices, barracks, gaols, prison camps – because all these are generally recognised as being *somewhere*, as actual parts of a person's life. No one writes about commuting (except incidentally) because no one sees it as a state or a predicament, as a valid experience.

Writers overlook the hours spent in the train in much the same way as most of them overlook the hours spent in the lavatory. They do not deliberately suppress the evidence. They simply never visualise themselves or their characters indulging in these mundane, time-consuming, and extremely formative activities as they waft from one adventure to the next. Their retrieval system just does not contain such data.

So commuting remains non-existent, *non terra non firma*, where it is not at, that which is not world, a hiatus, a lacuna, a vacuum, a gap, a blank, zilch, nowhere. If you look carefully, though, you may catch a glimpse of the real nature of commuting in the empty spaces between these notes. You may hear hints in the silence made by prose.

In guard's van, bundles of newspapers addressed to: Spook Erection, Moreton-in-Marsh Station.

Suddenly noticed how 'They' have shaped the tables like lids of children's coffins.

OVERHEARD 32
'Oxford's quite a good place because it's close to Birmingham.'

When 'They' allow the carefully phrased Passengers Travelling Second Class to use First Class carriages, 'They' first remove the antimacassars.

Once I laughed when in a second-hand bookshop I saw *The Inferno* on the travel shelf. Now I know better. Where, I wonder, will they decide to place Notebook? I should rejoice to find it not too far from the poetry shelf.

The Waste Line = *Le Train Vague*.

Clever new (to me, anyway) office plaything called viewfoil. You project a map, say, on to a screen. Then you can superimpose layer upon layer of plastic sheets which may show churches as red dots, cinemas as blue dots, footpaths as green lines – whatever you like. You can mark the spot with an X like Lawrence Durrell's quincunx.

The Premeditated Notebook uses the viewfoil system. So does a lot of poetry. Most novelists begin by trying to draw the underlying map. Poets and P.N. writers either assume the map as given, or accept that drawing the map lies beyond their capabilities. Instead, they work on preparing the sheets marked with dots or X or whatever, as beautifully and as accurately as they can. The reader then projects their viewfoils on to his map. With goodwill, endeavour, and a smattering of inspiration on either side, the result ought to be apocalyptic.

Dons waste a lot of time travelling in trains in order to waste more time sitting on committees with acronyms like CACTUS, OUCH and UGH.

Had I the leisure of Palinurus, I should enjoy at this stage taking time to compile a section on my *alter ego* Tiresias, 'who being blinde on earth sees more than all the rest in hell' (Thomas Browne), and on Thebes – 'the old childhood Thebes from which all the novels have issued' (Henry Miller). But commuting leaves no time for scholarship. These few hastily taken herbs and apples all I can offer.

HEADLINE (big deal) 14
Swindler Told To Pay Up £40.

OVERHEARD 33
1st Student: 'He's probably not as old as he looks.'
2nd Student (with great seriousness): 'Oh yes he is, he must be at least 23.'

Ah, Maidenhead allotments! I love to see you whizz,
A patchwork quilt of brassicas, beneath my passing phiz.

A curse on the train. Boulder which Sisyphus for ever heaves. Banquet which Tantalus never receives. Rotating wheel on which Ixion is castigated. Gyrating eagle by which Prometheus is lacerated. Eternal seat whence Theseus cannot move. Infernal beach where Palinurus must rove. Anathema sit.

Two and a half years ago I wondered how I should know when Notebook was finished. Now I have the answer –suddenly I just know that no more needs to be written – as simple as that. The identikit is complete. Appropriately or not, the moment has arrived during a train drivers' strike. I am sitting at home looking out at a sky full of snow and a landscape which grows whiter by the minute. They forecast a quick thaw.

Have been working on Notebook for about four years, at an average of about 14,000 words a year. Did not note date of first entry. Did not think of it then as the epochal event it has turned out to be for me. Notebook has sustained me all this time. I in turn have secretly sustained it and,

> Like the owner of a foul disease,
> To keep it from divulging, let it feed
> Even on the pith of life.

It has developed like a tumour, this long disease my book. Now must pluck up courage to ask the medical wallahs whether malignant or benign.

OXFORD STATION 6
VI
While he spoke on, I passed the barrier
Nor cast one lingering look behind,
Till at the first turning of the second street
I paused for breath,
Then sought with quiet heart my distant home.

Dear Notebook, I shall miss you. We have lived through a lot together, you and I. We have made hundreds of journeys – or rather, the same journey hundreds of times. We have seen dozens of commuters come and go. Have seen factories demolished and new ones built. Have seen thousands of trees die. Have witnessed the arrival of the bicycle and the departure of the crossword puzzle. Have weathered personal storms. Have . . . But no, I must stop before I wax maudlin-moral. There remains only one more thing to note, and that is the injunction which I used to see as a child, but did not then understand, in big white letters on a black ground, whenever I met or saw off my father at our local halt, namely:

Index